MORTGAGE

CONFIDENTIAL

MORTGAGE

CONFIDENTIAL

What You Need to Know That Your Lender Won't Tell You

David Reed

American Management Association

New York • Atlanta • Brussels • Chicago • Mexico City • San Francisco
Shanghai • Tokyo • Toronto • Washington, D.C.

Special discounts on bulk quantities of AMACOM books are available to corporations, professional associations, and other organizations. For details, contact Special Sales Department, AMACOM, a division of American Management Association, 1601 Broadway, New York, NY 10019.
Tel: 212-903-8316. Fax: 212-903-8083.
E-mail: specialsls@amanet.org
Website: www. amacombooks.org/go/specialsales
To view all AMACOM titles go to: www.amacombooks.org

This publication is designed to provide accurate and authoritative information in regard to the subject matter covered. It is sold with the understanding that the publisher is not engaged in rendering legal, accounting, or other professional service. If legal advice or other expert assistance is required, the services of a competent professional person should be sought.

REALTOR® is a registered collective membership mark that identifies a real estate professional who is a member of the NATIONAL ASSOCIATION of REALTORS® and subscribes to its strict code of ethics.

Library of Congress Cataloging-in-Publication Data

Reed, David (Carl David), 1957–
     Mortgage confidential : what you need to know that your lender won't tell you / David Reed.
     p. cm.
     Includes index.
     ISBN-13: 978-0-8144-7369-6
     ISBN-10: 0-8144-7369-5
     1. Mortgage loans.   I. Title.

HG2040.15.R443   2007
332.7′22—dc22

                                      2006025819

Printing number

10 9 8 7 6 5 4

To the loves of my life, my children:
Olivia, Benton, and Carter

Contents

Introduction

The mortgage process is extremely confusing. Besides the fact that there are lots of terms bandied about that are not used anywhere other than in home loans, there are so darned many people involved in the transaction. And these people have their own vocabulary. If you don't know what they're talking about, you are more susceptible to falling for things like:

Misleading marketing

Incomparable rate quotes

Bait and switch tactics

This is not to say that all lenders are crooks. Nor are all loan officers out to get you. Far from it. It's just that because the mortgage process is so bewildering and can happen so quickly, it's hard to catch up, much less understand the entire process.

The average loan officer might close 80 loans per year. That's a lot. But you might buy only two or three houses in your entire lifetime. That means that your loan officer does on a routine basis what you do on very, very rare occasions.

That's no different from other occupations. Anyone can have a unique specialty or trade. Certainly doctors and lawyers have their own protocols, terminology, and business practices. And so do mechanics.

And artists. And plumbers. In business life, everyone has something unique to her industry.

The difference is that while a mistake with a gardener might cost you fifty bucks for a new rosebush, a mistake on an interest rate could cost you thousands of dollars. Or qualifying for the wrong mortgage loan could mean that you're in over your head, which could cost you your home. You can get a new rosebush. You can't erase a foreclosure, and it's difficult to erase a bad mistake when it comes to a mortgage loan. That's why you need to know insider information—to protect yourself from costly mistakes and unethical loan officers.

Go to any bookstore and peruse the books on mortgages. How many of them were written by loan officers? Five? Two? One? Most home loan books are written by columnists or authors who have never filled out a home loan application other than their own.

They haven't compared rate sheets from one lender to the next. Or sat down and objectively compared one loan program with another at the behest of a new loan applicant.

I have. Not only do I write regular columns about home loans, but I have written two books specifically about mortgages. My first book, *Mortgages 101*, is a compendium of almost every mortgage question a consumer might have. My second book, *Who Says You Can't Buy a Home!*, is a consumer empowerment book that shows how people can buy properties every day, even though their situation might be considered, well, "challenged."

Mortgage Confidential now unveils information that is not commonly known by consumers so that they can decide what's right for them. Not only that, but *Mortgage Confidential* also pulls back the curtain on various loan officer practices that only the trained eye can identify.

I've seen almost every situation imaginable. I've seen people attempt to commit loan fraud—consumers and loan officers alike. I've watched the interest-rate market shake, rattle, and roll through various rate hikes and rate cuts.

Every so often I'll read a mortgage column in a popular newspaper or go online and look at what other people are writing about home loans. Now and then I'll read something and yell out loud, "That's wrong! You don't know what you're talking about!"

The thing about reading something that's been printed, whether it be in a newspaper column, in a magazine, or in a book, is that the reader automatically assumes that what has been printed is correct. That's not the case. And that's why those who aren't in the mortgage industry or those who just comment about it leave themselves open to error.

There are a lot of assumptions about mortgage financing that have reached urban myth status.

- Don't refinance your loan unless the rate is 2 percent below your current one. Wrong.
- If your credit score is below 620, you can get only a predatory loan. Wrong.
- You can't get a loan until your bankruptcy is seven years old. Wrong.
- You can't get a loan until your bankruptcy is two years old. Wrong again.
- The Fed controls your interest rate. Wrong.

And on, and on, and on.

This book will debunk all these myths and many more. Arm yourself with information, and you won't get taken. Read on.

Where Mortgage Loans Really Come From

The big myth about mortgage money has been around for a long, long time. It's about where the money comes from. Lenders don't make mortgage loans using money deposited by other customers. In fact, it's most likely that they borrow the money from somewhere else. This is called their *credit line*, and it is where mortgage bankers get their money.

Other mortgage companies don't actually make the loan at all; instead, they simply "arrange" the financing. This is called brokering. This is important, because if you don't understand how the lender makes its money, you won't understand where the pitfalls are.

By knowing how both a mortgage broker and a mortgage banker make money, you'll begin to get a glimpse of how each operates. This will help you uncover some of the mysteries of the mortgage process.

Your bank brokers. Your credit union brokers. Even your mortgage banker brokers. The main distinction in issuing mortgages is whether the loan application is taken by a mortgage broker who finds your loan for you or by a mortgage banker who has the money lying around somewhere and is anxious to lend that money to you as long as you pay it back on time and with a little interest, thank you very much.

Lenders make money in three basic ways:

1. They collect the money each month in the form of interest.
2. They make the money up front in junk fees, origination charges, and points.
3. They sell the loan, either at the time when your loan is being financed or later on down the road, to other lenders or investors who buy and sell mortgage loans.

Mortgage brokers make all their money up front. You won't send your broker any house payments, and your broker doesn't "sell" your mortgage. A common misperception is that a mortgage broker will sell your loan to a lender.

You'll see this statement made time and time again by people who don't know any better. You'll even hear mortgage brokers themselves talk about how they sell loans in order to make money. They say that they take a loan application, find a lender for you, and then sell your loan to that lender.

That's not what really happens. A mortgage broker doesn't "own" your loan. One can sell only something that one owns. Instead, a mortgage broker gets paid either by you or by the lender who provides your financing, or any combination of the two. But your loan is not sold. When you hear this term being bandied about by a mortgage broker, the broker is just trying to sound important. In fact, the broker may be important, but it's not because he has the ability to sell your loan to the highest bidder (or the lowest, for that matter).

A mortgage banker funds mortgages using its own money. A mortgage broker does not. A mortgage banker may sell your loan to someone else or keep it because it owns the loan. Mortgage bankers include the retail banks that you see on nearly every street corner and credit unions.

Mortgage bankers make money by making loans, but first they have to have the money in order to lend it, right? Guess what? They borrow it from other lenders or establish a credit line at their bank or with other investors. Your bank doesn't open up its vault, raid its customers' piggy banks, and use those funds to make a mortgage loan.

If you're getting your mortgage from your mortgage banker or bank and you think that your loyalty to it is a deciding factor in the loan approval, you're wrong. Mortgage bankers can borrow the money they need in one lump sum at a negotiated interest rate, park that money in an interest-bearing account, and begin issuing mortgage loans one loan at a time.

Let's say a credit line is available at 3.00 percent. A lender will arrange that financing, then turn around and issue mortgage loans.

An individual loan officer at that mortgage company will find a borrower for her employer. For example, a buyer wants a 30-year fixed-rate loan and gets it at 6.75 percent. The lender transfers the money from its credit line to make the mortgage. The lender can keep that mortgage and collect the monthly payments in the form of interest each month based upon the loan amount and the rate on that loan.

The lender does this over and over again, month after month, and makes money in the form of interest.

Or the lender can decide to sell that loan to someone else. Lenders can make money by finding someone else who is willing to pay a certain amount of money to buy loans. How much do loans cost? Whatever the market decides, but typically your banker will make a 1 percent "commission" on each loan. If a lender sells $100 million in mortgages to someone else, the lender will immediately make $1 million and not have to wait for it in the form of monthly payments.

For instance, a 30-year mortgage loan at 7.00 percent on $200,000 gives you a monthly payment of $1,330 per month. Over 30 years, that loan yields just over $279,000, in addition to paying back the original $200,000 borrowed. That's a lot of money.

CONFIDENTIAL: Odds Are, Your Mortgage Will Be Sold

A lender can decide to make money on a particular loan by collecting interest each and every month, or it can sell that loan for a single payment to a willing buyer. That $200,000 loan at 7.00 percent has a potential return of $279,000. That's the value if the loan is held for the full 30 years, which quite frankly doesn't happen that often.

But still, there is considerable value in that note. That's why lenders sell loans. And selling a loan also frees up more money to make yet another mortgage. That process can be repeated over and over again, and in fact often is.

Whether or not a mortgage company sells your loan is purely a business decision based upon how active that mortgage company is in the market. If a mortgage banker is feeling aggressive about the mortgage market and is ready to make a few bucks, it contacts its legion of loan officers and tells them to go out and sell new loans.

Why do some lenders sell loans, while at the same time others buy them? Why buy a loan when you can just go out and make one instead? The practice is called *originating* a mortgage loan. When a loan officer finds a home loan, that loan is originated by that person.

But that loan officer doesn't come cheap. Nor does the building he works in and the people who help process the loan. Nor does all the insurance the banker pays for along with the electricity bill, payroll, and— well, you get the picture. It costs a lot of money to find a loan. Some lenders will forgo the originating process and simply buy loans from other lenders and collect the monthly interest.

Why the difference? It depends upon a multitude of things, but primarily it rests on the current focus of the lending institution. A mortgage is a solid investment. People do everything they can to keep their homes by making their payments on time. Banks like that.

This steady rate of return allows banks and other lenders to strategize their business plan. If a lender knows that it will get X percent each and every month, that helps it develop new marketing strategies and provides needed stability when it decides to invest in other ventures, such as a shopping center or a small business loan.

It surprises some people to learn that their bank or credit union has sold their loan to someone else, often to someone that they've never heard of. And many times it leaves people feeling betrayed by their own bank.

In fact, the odds are that your loan will be sold to someone else at some point in time.

CONFIDENTIAL: Not Only Can Your Bank Sell Your Mortgage, but You Gave It Permission to Do So

When you visit your bank, notice all those cheery people in those posters that line your bank's walls with sayings like "Let us be your home loan lender!" or "You're our customer and our Number 1 priority!" or some such.

Because you have your checking account, your savings account, your auto loan, and probably a credit card at your bank, you feel comfortable there. After all, your bank is your friend, right? At least, that's what the posters say.

So you decide to get a home loan at your bank. You move in, and then a few weeks later, you get a notice saying, "Your Bank has just sold your loan to Big Mortgage Company. Thank you for letting us serve you."

This is a surprising secret that most consumers don't know about. Consumers can feel let down or even lied to when their bank sells their home loan. After all, if you wanted your mortgage to be from Big Mortgage Company, you would have applied there in the first place, right? Of course.

But guess what? You did know about it. At least, you signed a piece of paper claiming that you knew about it. How's that? Surprised?

Federal law requires mortgage companies to disclose two things to you regarding selling your loan:

1. Whether or not your loan will be sold
2. What percentage of the loans that your lender issues will be sold

Trust me. You signed this. I fully understand that you signed maybe 20 documents of various types when you applied for a home loan, but this is one that you signed. The problem with these disclosures is that consumers may not be aware of what exactly is going on, primarily because of the language used to tell the borrower that the loan could be sold.

The obscure terminology used is "servicing rights." A loan servicer is the organization that you send your payments to, and the form you signed is called the servicing disclosure. Your potential lender is required to tell you what percentage of its loans it sold last year to other investors. This is usually done by checking a box, such as 0–25%, 26–50%, 51–75%, or 76–100%.

So should you feel betrayed because your bank sold your loan to someone else? You could. In fact, when your bank sells your loan suddenly, there might be some other unexpected consequences that you didn't count on.

CONFIDENTIAL: If Your Bank Sells Your Loan, You May Lose Some Privileges

A few years ago, I took out a mortgage loan that went to my bank. Because I had my mortgage and my credit card with my bank, I suddenly got free checking, a free safe deposit box, and reduced fees and rates on various bank offerings. I even got cashier's checks and notary services at no charge—all because my mortgage was with my bank. After about a year of financial bank bliss, I was informed that my loan had been sold to another bank where I had no accounts at all.

Guess what? That's right. Since my mortgage was no longer with my original bank because the bank had sold it, I also lost all of those freebies I originally had. And that bugged me. It could bug you, too, but the very fact that your loan can be sold in the first place yields a greater benefit: lower rates.

CONFIDENTIAL: Sometimes Your Rate Is Not Reduced When You Pay Points

Mortgage bankers can also make money up front, at the initial loan application, in the form of various "junk" fees, discount points, or origination charges.

A discount point is a percentage of a loan amount: 1 "point" is equal to 1 percent of the loan you're about to take. Thus, 1 point on $300,000 is $3,000, 2 points is $6,000, and so on. The term *discount points* is sometimes used because points represent a percentage of the loan and are used to lower the interest rate on that loan.

Points are nothing more than prepaid interest on a mortgage. You pay the lender its interest ahead of time, at the beginning of your new loan, and in exchange you get a slightly lower interest rate. Normally 1 discount point will reduce your rate by about $1/4$ percent. Normally.

The fact is that mortgage lenders can charge you pretty much anything they can get away with and still be competitive in the marketplace. A lender might charge you 3 points, but these might not be discount points because your rate is not reduced accordingly. If an interest rate of 8.00 percent is available at 1 point, then 7.75 percent should be available for 2 points. If this is your situation, you're paying a discount point.

Sometimes lenders will charge you points and not reduce the rate at all. In this case, you're getting no discount whatsoever. To see if this is happening to you, ask your lender for various rate and point quotes—say, everything from 6.00 percent to 7.00 percent. For each $^1/_4$ percent change in rate, you should see 1 point. If you're not seeing that spread, ask your loan officer to sharpen his pencil and do the math again.

CONFIDENTIAL: Some Fees Are Junk Fees

Lenders also make money on origination charges. In some parts of the country (California, for example), origination charges are uncommon, but they are common in most places. An origination fee is also usually expressed as a percentage of the loan amount. A 1 percent origination fee on a $250,000 loan is $2,500. A 2 percent fee is $5,000.

Finally, lenders make money on junk fees, so called because they don't go directly to pay for any particular product or service. When you pay $15 for a credit report and get, well, a credit report, you're getting a product or service.

What you're getting for a junk fee is sometimes obscure. Common junk fees may be called administration fees or commitment fees. You'll also see application fees, broker fees, or processing charges. We'll discuss closing cost in greater detail in Chapter 4, but charging junk fees at the time of application is still another way that mortgage companies can make money on a loan.

This third method of making money on a loan, charging fees at the time of the loan application, is the way mortgage brokers make money. The mortgage broker can charge you a processing fee and/or an origination fee, but it does not make money by selling loans or collecting monthly payments.

CONFIDENTIAL: Mortgage Brokers Must Tell You How Much They're Making on Your Loan

One interesting difference between mortgage brokers and mortgage bankers is that brokers are required by law to tell you exactly how much money they're going to make and who's going to pay them.

When you apply for a mortgage loan, mortgage brokers have a legal obligation to not only discuss the closing costs you'll encounter, but also tell you where their income is coming from. This is disclosed on a disclosure form called the Good Faith Estimate of Settlement Charges.

Most mortgage brokers will tell you that it's certainly no secret to them that they're required to tell the consumer how much money they're going to make off of her. It's a contentious issue with them. And their industry has been fighting this provision for years now, claiming that the mortgage broker is the only party in a typical real estate transaction that has to disclose how much money it's making.

CONFIDENTIAL: Wholesale Lenders Can Pay Brokers to Send Them Loans

Mortgage brokers don't lend money; they find money. And they find money from a group of mortgage companies called *wholesale lenders*.

Wholesale lenders don't make loans to consumers directly. Instead, they make loan programs available to mortgage brokers, who in turn "mark up" the interest rate to the retail level. The difference between the wholesale rate and the marked-up rate is how much money the broker makes. It's not unlike any other wholesale/retail consumer product: Buy low, sell high.

Brokers can make more money on your loan with something called a yield spread premium, or YSP. Each morning, all wholesale lenders publish their interest rates for that business day. And while most of these rates will be the same, there might be a difference in how much each interest rate "costs" the mortgage broker.

For example, a mortgage broker will begin comparing interest rates from various wholesale lenders. The forte of a mortgage broker is that the broker has the ability to "shop" for the best mortgage rate by comparing the hundreds of lenders that the broker is signed up with.

But what the broker may really be doing is not finding you the best rate but finding himself the most money.

A broker can peruse the daily wholesale rate offerings and find three lenders offering a 15-year fixed-rate mortgage at 5.50 percent. The difference is not the rate; the difference may be the YSP.

Lender A might offer a 1.00 percent YSP, Lender B might be offering a 1.375 percent YSP, while Lender C is offering only 0.875 percent that day, all on the very same 15-year fixed-rate mortgage program. Remember, it's the YSP that typically goes to the mortgage broker as its profit. So which lender do you think the broker is going to choose? Lender B.

On a $400,000 loan, Lender A pays the broker $4,000, Lender B pays $5,500, while Lender C can muster only $3,500 that day. Lender B gets your loan because the broker makes more money from it while you get the rate you were promised.

Is that mortgage broker going to give you back some of that money? No. Should she? I don't think so, but others may disagree. If you agreed to a 5.50 percent interest rate and your broker locked you in at that rate, then you got what you wanted. Of course, a mortgage broker who picks up a few extra bucks because she found a slightly better deal at one of her wholesale lenders could certainly offer to give you some of that "extra" money (we'll look at that more closely in Chapter 5), but she is not obligated to. Compare it to a retail store. If the store can cut its costs on a product, it can pass along the savings to you, but it is not obligated to do that.

CONFIDENTIAL: YSPs Are Not Bad for the Consumer

Is there something the matter with YSPs? Is the wholesale lender paying the broker to place a mortgage loan with it?

Some people claim that the yield spread premium amounts to nothing more than one lender bribing a mortgage broker to send your loan to it by paying the mortgage broker a sizable YSP. But to claim that a consumer gets an unfair rate simply because of the existence of a YSP is not accurate.

There is absolutely no doubt that the YSP can be abused, but so can any loan product. If you can get the very same loan program down the street, but at a rate that is $1/4$ to $1/2$ percent better, your loan officer is taking advantage of you and abusing the system. A loan program itself is not bad simply because of the existence of a YSP.

When you get a rate quote from a mortgage broker, or any lender, for that matter, and the rate quoted has no points and no origination charges, the only way a loan officer can make a profit is through a YSP. Without YSPs, mortgage rates overall would be higher for the consumer because there would be less competition in the mortgage market. If a broker can't offer a no-points loan just like his counterparts in the mortgage banking industry, then there is less competition. Less competition in the mortgage marketplace means higher rates.

Mortgage brokers can't find interest rates that are significantly lower than those offered by anyone else in the market. They can't. It's impossible. Okay, a broker might find a rate that is $1/8$ percent or sometimes even $1/4$ percent lower than what you can get from your mortgage banker, but what brokers certainly can't do is find a loan that is $1/2$ percent or more better than anyone else in the marketplace.

So if a mortgage broker finds a competitive loan program from a wholesale lender, who exactly is this lender, anyway, and are you sure you'll like the lender that the mortgage broker found for you?

Sometimes a mortgage broker keeps this information secret for as long as it can. It does this for three reasons:

1. The broker is afraid that you'll bypass him entirely and go directly to the lender making the loan.
2. He hasn't officially locked you in, although he told you that he has.
3. He doesn't have the loan or rate you're looking for, but he has told you that he has, and he is frantically searching for it.

Mortgage brokers' prime ingredient is the knowledge they have. Their job is to scour various lenders' offerings each and every day to find the best rates, the best service, the loan programs, and so on.

Mortgage brokers apply to a mortgage company's wholesale division in order to begin doing business with that wholesale lender. A mortgage broker must be approved by a wholesale lender in order to market mortgage loans for that lender. Almost every mortgage company you've ever heard of has a wholesale division. My bank has a wholesale division, and probably your bank does too if it's one of the top 50 banks in the United States.

These wholesale divisions recruit mortgage brokers to market their loan products for them. So, each day an account representative from the wholesale lender makes sales calls all day long to different mortgage brokers in his area for the sole purpose of recruiting new brokers.

Each wholesale lender will market itself much the way a broker would: "Send us your loans because we have great rates, great service, blah, blah . . ." or "We have a loan program designed specifically for second-time buyers . . ." or whatever.

The mortgage broker will make an application to the wholesale lender to be one of its brokers. The wholesale lender will require that the broker be duly licensed in the state he does business in, that he have a minimum net worth (sometimes), that his office not be a den of thieves, and so on.

It is to a mortgage broker's advantage to sign with as many wholesale lenders as possible because maybe, just maybe, one particular lender will offer an interest rate that pays a lot more money than other wholesale lenders will.

CONFIDENTIAL: Brokers May Try to Keep Who the Lender Is a Secret Until the End

Often your mortgage broker will keep quiet about who your lender is going to be, especially if the broker thinks you might skip the broker altogether and go directly to the lender itself. Makes sense, right?

I'll give you an example. A few years ago a well-known lender had a program that was unlike any other in the market. It was designed for doctors who were fresh out of medical school and fresh out of money after paying for medical school. This loan program allowed for the newly christened doctor to buy a home with no money down under a preferred loan program. This program not only was available in the retail sector (bank direct), but was also made available to its legion of mortgage brokers.

One particular mortgage broker got a list of recent medical graduates from the local medical school and sent those doctors a letter explaining this program. He got lots of responses and took lots of loan applications, but he never told his borrowers who the lender was until the very last minute.

He was afraid that the doctors would go directly to the bank and bypass him altogether. After all, he had done the hard work of finding the mailing list, putting together a marketing campaign, and taking all those new loan applications.

Fair enough. But there are two problems when this happens. First, mortgage brokers get their loan programs on a wholesale basis, so the doctor wouldn't be saving any money by going directly to the lender, and second, suppose the doctor hated that bank's guts and would never do business with that bank for the rest of her life, regardless of any loan program.

Does that sound silly? Not if you've had to go round and round with your bank, with funds not properly applied to your account, or your mortgage payments being counted as late when they were not and being reported to the credit bureau.

Some lenders have run afoul of the law or have been penalized by the federal government for unfair lending practices or discrimination. Consumers read this stuff and can have as many reasons not to use a particular bank or lender as there are stars in the sky.

This happened to me several years ago when a particular lender made the papers for totally messing up its servicing portfolio. A borrower told me that she didn't care where her loan went as long as it wasn't to *that* lender.

Still, mortgage brokers can keep this information secret. Many don't, but some do. If the broker doesn't tell you, it's because the broker doesn't trust you. Don't work with a broker who doesn't trust you. Trust works both ways, right?

CONFIDENTIAL: Your Broker May Not Know Until the End Who Will Ultimately Be Your Lender

Another reason mortgage brokers won't tell you who the lender is that they haven't yet decided where your loan is going to go. So far, no big deal. If you haven't decided to lock in your loan, then the broker won't know who your lender will eventually be. But he'll have a pretty good idea because he will use only a handful of lenders on a regular basis, not the hundreds he may be authorized to do business with.

"Your loan will probably go to XZ Bank, 123 Bank, or ABC Lending Company, but I haven't decided which," says your broker. That's the answer you want to hear.

CONFIDENTIAL: If You Locked in a Rate and Your Broker Can't Tell You Who the Lender Is, She's Lying

On the other hand, if in fact you have locked in your rate, but your broker hasn't told you who the lender is, then there's a problem, and one that you need to watch out for. Of course, this could be a symptom of the first type of paranoia: The broker doesn't want you to go directly to the lender.

More likely, you have locked in the rate with the mortgage broker, but the broker hasn't officially locked you in with the wholesale lender. We'll discuss rate lock tricks in greater detail in Chapter 5, but if this happens to you, then you need to prepare yourself and ask some direct questions.

"Mr. Mortgage Broker, I would like to lock in today at 5.00 percent."

"Great!" says the broker. "I'll lock you right after we get off the phone!"

A couple of days later you call your broker to confirm your lock.

"Rates have gone up since we last spoke. You locked me in at 5.00 percent like I asked, right?"

"Yes, you're locked in at 5.00 percent."

"Great, thanks. Who is my lender?"

"Um . . ." (Uh-oh.)

Guess what? I'll bet you a fresh doughnut you're not locked in. It's likely that your broker either forgot to lock you in or told you that you were locked in but decided to "play the market" (discussed in detail in Chapter 5), and now the rate is nowhere to be found. The broker is hoping that rates will come back down so that she can lock you in.

CONFIDENTIAL: Beware of "Special" Deals

Just as an unheard-of interest rate may be quoted to you simply to get your loan application, a similar game can be played when it comes to loan programs. The program offered is not just any loan program, but a program that carries some unique qualifying features—qualifying features that not many lenders offer. If any do.

I'll give you an example. A guy wanted to begin investing in real estate. Rates were low, property values were on the rise, and he thought he wanted to make it big in the real estate business. But he had a slight problem: He didn't have any money. Or at least, he had the money, but didn't want to use it.

So he began his search for a mortgage that would allow him to buy a rental house with no money down. He found a few lenders that offered such a program. Then he began to fine-tune his search a little further. His new challenge was that his income wasn't sufficient to carry the mortgages on the new houses unless those homes were being rented. He needed the rental income in order to qualify.

That's a big problem. Most such real estate investment loans require that the buyer have previous experience in being a landlord. Two years' experience is a common requirement for most investment loans. This experience is usually verified by examining the loan applicant's tax returns to see whether any rental income was reported and/or whether depreciation was counted against any real estate.

This buyer didn't have any landlord experience. None. That automatically disqualified him from these loan programs. He had to start all over again.

This time he researched mortgage loans that did not have a requirement of experience as a landlord and at the same time did not require a down payment. He found a handful of lenders and a couple of mortgage brokers that had such a program. Relieved, he began to make a loan application at a lender and at the broker.

Yet another problem arose. The loan programs he found didn't require a down payment or landlord experience, but they did require that he have six months' worth of house payments sitting in the bank, liquid. He didn't have a down payment, much less six months' worth of payments. Dejected, he gave up.

The next day, he got a call from a broker. "I've found a lender that will do what you want, but it's a little more expensive than you wanted. It costs 3 points. Do you want to proceed?"

The customer decided to go ahead and invest, thinking that finally owning a rental property would help him qualify more easily down the road when he wanted to buy more rental houses.

But the broker didn't reveal his source. After all the phone calls and all the research the customer had done on his own, plus all the research all the other lenders and mortgage brokers did, this broker had found the one loan program he could use.

Or had she?

The loan officer was evasive when the customer asked for more details. The terms of the note were not fully disclosed, and the lender certainly wasn't identified.

"The lender quotes on such loans only after review of the loan application and the credit report. I'll need to get your loan application, along with money for your credit report and an application fee."

The customer didn't bite. It sounded too fishy. In fact, there was no lender; the loan officer was trying to get a loan application and some money from the borrower and then would either continue searching for the required loan program or get the client to the very end and change loan programs—long after the buyer had already paid for appraisals, inspections, and application fees.

If your broker has some loan program that no one else has—and I mean no one—don't go for it unless he's able to tell you who the lender will be and quote you rational loan terms. Don't give in to the temptation to believe that you've found the holy mortgage grail. You could very well lose lots of money, as well as your pride.

CONFIDENTIAL: Many Mortgage Bankers Allow Their Loan Officers to Broker Loans

Many mortgage bankers allow their loan officers to broker out a mortgage from a wholesale lender if they don't offer a competing product.

Let's say that a new loan program hits the market that all the mortgage brokers are raving about. This is a common occurrence; a mortgage wholesale company tries to think up new loan programs that will attract new mortgage brokers who will bring it new business.

A real-world example might be the payment option loan program (discussed in Chapter 7) that made headlines not too long ago. Suddenly, this new loan program hit the streets with great fanfare. Loan officers working for other mortgage bankers that didn't offer that program yelled at their bosses, saying that they were getting creamed on the streets by their competitors, who could offer this new loan program. They asked repeatedly why they didn't have a program just like it.

In cases like these, the mortgage banker may let a loan officer send the loan to a wholesale lender, just like a regular broker would do. Instead of losing the deal altogether, by brokering the loan to a wholesale lender, the loan officer and the banker make a little more money, and the banker has one more happy customer.

In fact, brokering loans is more common than you might think. Mortgage loans that are brokered make up over half of all loans issued in this country—possibly more than that, depending upon which source you read. And they're not all originated by a fully licensed, official mortgage broker.

One of the more common mortgage brokers is your credit union. Many credit unions don't operate like a mortgage banker, with their own credit lines, but instead broker out their mortgages. Sure, they may take your loan application, quote you interest rates, and make you sign lots of papers, but they're acting like a mortgage broker. This is especially true if your credit union is local and not a national organization.

CONFIDENTIAL: Mortgage Brokers May Be Able to Find, on Any Given Day, a Slightly Better Rate Quote

Or so it seems. We'll discuss rates in more detail in Chapter 5, but the fact is that rates are mostly the same, give or take a bit, wherever you go.

The difference is that on any given day, some lenders will be better than other lenders. Not by a lot, maybe by $1/8$ percent or so in rate. But it's still enough to make a difference. Your job is to make sure that your broker is giving you the best rate possible and that this rate beats anything you can get at other lenders.

How much is that $1/8$ percent? On a $200,000 mortgage paid over 30 years at 6.00 percent, your monthly payment would be $1,199. At $6^1/8$ percent, your monthly payment goes to $1,215. That's not a lot, mind you, but it's enough to notice. That's $16 you'll be saving each and every month, and if you're one of those who plan on keeping the loan to its full term, then that's 30 years times 12 months times $16, or $5,760.

Even if it's not in the rate, $^1/_8$ percent also yields a discount point reduction of $^1/_2$ point. If you can get 6.00 percent at 1 discount point, then 6.125 percent should cost you only $^1/_2$ point. On that same $200,000, that $^1/_2$ point results in a $1,000 savings.

That's where a broker can help. Don't expect to get 6.00 percent while everyone else is getting 7.00 percent, but you can often times find a slightly better rate.

CONFIDENTIAL: Mortgage Brokers Aren't More Expensive Than Mortgage Bankers

At least, they shouldn't be. There's a common misperception that mortgage brokers are nothing more than middlemen who get paid for finding a mortgage loan that the consumer couldn't find on her own. Because they're middlemen, the argument goes, they mark the loan up higher than retail. But that's simply not the case.

Yes, there certainly are times when brokers can charge excessive fees, origination charges, and points, but that's abusive and probably predatory. Predatory lending practices will be revealed in Chapter 6.

Brokers get their mortgage programs at rates below the market, add their margin to the product, then price that product at a competitive enough rate to hopefully originate the loan.

CONFIDENTIAL: Your Mortgage Broker Doesn't Use 100 Lenders

So how many wholesale lenders do mortgage brokers actually deal with? If you believe their advertisements or read the material from one of their brochures, they're set up with hundreds, and I mean hundreds, of lenders. You've seen the advertisements.

"We have access to over 100 national banks and mortgage companies
. . . let us find the right program for you!"

But do you think your loan officer will actually go pore through literally thousands of interest rates just to find you the best deal? Of course
not; he'd be spending all of his time looking at rate sheets and wouldn't
have time to take care of his customers.

Mortgage brokers tout how many lenders they're signed up with, and
a broker might in fact be signed up with 100 different mortgage lenders,
or more, but she won't use them all. She'll probably use only a handful.

When I started out in the mortgage business as a mortgage broker, I
spent tons of time going through rate sheets. After a few weeks of this, I
finally began to notice something. I probably spent a total of 100 + hours
looking at rate sheets when I first got into the business, only to discover
that . . . *everybody's rates are the same!*

So what did I do? Like every other mortgage broker you'll ever meet
that's been in the business for very long, I quit going through those rate
sheets—at least, all 100 of them. Instead, your mortgage broker probably
just looks at the ones from companies that he's used to doing business
with. There's no need to waste so much time; all the loan officer needs to
do is pick up the rate sheets from his favorite lenders, compare them, and
move on.

It's those lenders that he'll compare to find that extra $1/8$ percent that
he hopes to either quote to you to get your deal or use to make a little
extra money from the deal.

"We're signed up with 100 lenders" is nothing more than a marketing
pitch. A broker may in fact be signed up with that many, but there's really
no way for you to go through your mortgage broker's wholesale lender
file cabinet and count them. You just have to have a level of trust in this
instance. And if the broker does have 100 or more lenders, she's probably
not going to look at all of them every day.

CONFIDENTIAL: Sometimes the Best Rate Is Not Your Only Consideration

If brokers have access to more programs and can search for better deals, then why doesn't everybody use a broker?

The benefit from using a mortgage banker is the control he has over the loan process. When there is a problem with a loan file (and problems happen every minute of the day), you want your lender to be a banker, not a broker.

Just as a mortgage broker may have 100 lenders at her disposal, each of those wholesale lenders has hundreds of loan files sitting on his desk—all from different brokers. Whereas a mortgage broker might close 10 loans per month, a wholesale lender might close that many in a single minute.

Why do bankers fix problems more quickly than brokers? First, because they have direct access to their own files. A broker does not; she has to call the wholesale lender to get things fixed, all the while going through additional channels.

Here's how it works. A broker submits a loan file to a wholesale lender. Each day, the wholesale lender logs the files it receives, then distributes them to its underwriters. These underwriters are also still working on loans given to them the day before. And if the wholesale lender is doing its job right, more loans are coming through that door at a brisk clip.

This broker's file is about to be underwritten, and it is assigned a loan number. Later that day, or longer if the lender is really busy (I've seen underwriting take five to seven days before a decision is issued), the loan goes to the underwriter for sign-off.

But wait: The underwriter notices that the borrower has two last names in her credit report. This might indicate that she was previously married. So the underwriter stops what he's doing and e-mails, calls, or contacts the wholesale lender's account executive that services that particular mortgage broker.

The account executive calls the loan processor and says, "Your applicant has two last names on her credit report. Do you know if she's been married before or is known by any other name? Can we get that cleared up?"

At first glance, this isn't any big deal, right? So what if she had two last names? What does that matter; she still qualifies for the loan, right?

Actually, maybe not. Two names on a female's credit report can indicate a previous marriage. Was she married to Mr. Smith, got divorced, and now uses her maiden name, Ms. Jones? If she was in fact divorced, the underwriter will want to see her divorce decree, because the divorce decree will show whether she is obligated to pay any spousal or child support, which could affect her debt ratios.

I'm not kidding here; this happens every day somewhere in the lending business.

But the communication chain to get all this straightened out is jumbled up. First, the underwriter calls the account executive, and the account executive calls the loan processor or loan officer. The loan officer tracks down the borrower and asks her, "Were you known as Mrs. Smith at some point, or have you ever been married and are now divorced?"

Ms. Jones answers, "Yes, I was married to that idiot; what's wrong now?"

The broker says, "We need a copy of your divorce decree so that we can establish that you have no financial obligations to your ex."

"That was six years ago. I don't have that decree, and I don't know where to get it."

"We'll have to find the judge, the court records, your attorney, just someone who might have a copy of it. There's no way around this."

"Okay," says Ms. Jones and hangs up the phone. Now things come to a screeching halt. Gotta find that divorce decree. After several days and more than a few phone calls, Ms. Jones calls back and says, "Okay, I found a copy. I'm going to bring it over."

The divorce decree is delivered to the mortgage broker. It is then sent via overnight courier to the lender, who logs it in (along with all the other new loan files that have been delivered for approval by other mortgage brokers) and puts it in line to be reviewed by the underwriter who originally asked to clear up the name discrepancy.

So far, this process has taken several days—not just because the borrower had to track down old papers, but because there is an ongoing time lag between the mortgage broker and the underwriter who approved the loan. When there are problems with a loan file, this "wall" between a broker and a lender can be a challenge. And it can make the difference between your deal going through or not.

This same scenario with a banker works a little differently.

The loan is submitted to the underwriter, which typically means that the loan moves from one part of the office to another. Even if it goes to another building or another town, it's still the same lender.

The underwriter picks up the file and begins underwriting. He sees that there's a discrepancy in the credit file. Instead of putting everything on hold, he calls the loan officer directly.

"David, your client has two last names on her credit report. What gives?"

"I didn't notice that. I'll call her. Hold on."

"Ms. Jones, there are two last names on your credit report. Have you been married and divorced?"

"Yes, I've been married and divorced."

"Do you pay any monthly alimony or support payments?"

"No"

"Do you have a copy of your divorce decree?"

"No; that was six years ago."

"Hold on."

"Underwriter, she's been divorced, and she doesn't have a copy of her divorce decree to establish whether or not she has additional monthly obligations. How else can we make this determination?" David asks.

"If we could get a copy of all of her bank statements and we don't find any consistent monthly payments that we can't account for, then I could sign off on that. Her loan application says she has one dependent. If we can get a copy of her tax returns showing that she has received child support payments as income, then I'll be satisfied about her obligations and we can approve the loan."

"Hold on."

"Ms. Jones, you show one dependent on your loan application. Is this dependent from your previous marriage?"

"Yes."

"Can you get me 12 months' bank statements?"

"Yes, I can do that right now."

"Mr. Underwriter, I have bank statements, tax returns, and a borrower's written statement that she is not obligated to pay support, she is the one receiving support payments, and we can document that."

"Great," says the underwriter. "We're good to go."

I can relate this story because it happened to me several years ago. Because I was the loan officer with the mortgage banker, I was able to discuss an alternative loan condition directly with the underwriter.

If I had been a broker trying to do the same thing, it would have taken days just to get a copy of the divorce decree. I wouldn't have had direct access to the underwriter to get problems worked out. I would have had to go through the "system" to get my documentation in front of the lender for review.

This change of control was crystal clear to me when I moved from San Diego to Austin in 1995. While I was in San Diego, I was a mortgage broker. When I moved to Texas, I began as a loan officer for a mortgage banker.

As a broker, sending a loan file was almost like sending one of my kids on the school bus for the very first time. I knew I had done everything right, but somehow I had lost control. My child was not just mine alone any longer; he was one of hundreds of kids at school. Yeah, I could call the school if there was a problem, but it wasn't the same.

As a banker, I could call the shots at each and every turn. Approval? Yep, got it. Draw closing papers? Pick up the phone. Fund the loan? Ditto. Pure control. I loved it. Yes, as a broker, I could search for a slightly better rate; maybe I would find it and maybe I wouldn't. But the pure peace of mind is worth much more.

I want to season this story with a couple of thoughts. A mortgage broker who has been in business for a long time and has established a reputation in the mortgage industry as a knowledgeable, fair, and competent person has greater access to wholesale lenders and their staff than other brokers who send in an occasional mortgage loan.

But when there are problems with a mortgage loan, mortgage bankers generally can make a decision on the fly. Brokers have to go through too many channels to reach the same level of efficiency.

CONFIDENTIAL: Your Best Choice May Not Be Either a Broker or a Banker

There's a third option open to borrowers called *correspondent lending*. And it mixes the best of both the mortgage broker and the mortgage banker.

A mortgage banker who acts as a correspondent does so by agreeing to send a loan that she originates to the corresponding lender right after money changes hands. In this instance, a mortgage loan is truly "sold" and is done so individually. Selling a single loan to another lender is called *flow* selling. Flow selling is simply selling the rights to a loan as the loan gets funded.

But here's the neat part. Just as a mortgage broker can shop around for the right loan at the right price, so too can a mortgage banker shop around for the very same loan and price with different mortgage bankers who have correspondent relationships with one another.

In this instance, a mortgage banker will originate the loan, search for a competitive rate quote from another mortgage banker (just as a broker would do with a wholesale lender), lock in the rate, document the loan, approve it, and issue a mortgage using its very own funds.

When you apply for a mortgage with one of these bankers and lock in your loan, the mortgage banker in turn immediately locks in that loan with its correspondent lender. By locking it in, the mortgage banker has "presold" that loan to the corresponding lender at a set price, determined ahead of time. When the loan is funded, it is then shipped to the correspondent lender.

Just as a wholesale lender offers below-market rates to mortgage brokers, so do correspondent lenders offer below-market pricing to their mortgage bankers. Almost every time, this price is even lower than what wholesale lenders can offer their mortgage brokers.

The correspondent banker also performs other specific functions that the mortgage broker is not set up to provide. Brokers can't underwrite loan files or sign off on mortgage loan approval conditions; they can't print closing papers; they certainly can't issue funds for the loan because they're not bankers; and they don't ship the loan to the wholesale mortgage lender who granted the mortgage in the first place. (We'll address the various people in the loan process in the next chapter.)

In exchange for a correspondent banker's taking on all of this additional loan overhead in the form of salaries and jobs, a lower rate is given. How much lower is this rate? A common exchange is usually another $1/4$ to $1/2$ point.

Correspondent bankers can not only search for a lower rate, but also search for a particular loan program that not all lenders offer.

A national mortgage banker is mostly stuck with whatever loan programs his company is offering, and with the rates and terms listed on its rate sheet. If a loan officer at one of these large mortgage bankers discovers that her rates on 15-year fixed-rate loans are out of the market by $1/4$ percent, then she's out of luck. She has to use what she has on her rate sheet.

Correspondent mortgage bankers operate like brokers when pricing and searching for loan programs.

You've never heard of a correspondent mortgage banker? Me neither until I became one. Yes, I lived in my own little mortgage broker world and didn't know any better, but I was actually floored when I found that not only did I have access to almost every loan program in the market, but I had very, very competitive interest rates. I had the best of both worlds when I became a correspondent mortgage banker.

If you've never heard of correspondent bankers, then how in the world do you find them? Most correspondent bankers are smaller, regional players in the mortgage industry. You have to first find a mortgage banker by asking him if he is in fact a banker or a broker. If he's a banker, ask him if he works with correspondent lenders. First, the person on the other end of the phone will be surprised that you even know what a correspondent lender is, so he'll assume that you're in the business or know someone who is.

If he says yes, then you've definitely found someone you want to get some mortgage offers from. And just as you would ask a mortgage broker whom she does business with, ask the banker whom he does business with. He'll tell you.

Common wholesale and correspondent lenders are Bank of America, Countrywide, GMAC, and Chase. There are countless others, some with names you'd know and others that you wouldn't know.

Is a correspondent lender always going to be your best choice? There are a myriad of reasons to use a particular lender. Some consumers won't touch a mortgage company they've never heard of. Some like to get their mortgage at the same place where they have their checking account. Others have special requirements that demand the specific tools that a broker has. At the same time, a correspondent banker won't always have a lower rate than everyone else. The rate might be the same as all the other quotes you're getting, or it might be higher, depending upon how much money the loan officer wants to make off of your loan.

However, all things being equal between a mortgage broker, a mortgage banker, and a correspondent banker: hands down, the correspondent lender is your best choice in terms of the price of the loan and the control that the lender has over the loan process.

CONFIDENTIAL: Fannie Mae, Freddie Mac, the VA, and the FHA Don't Make Loans

You hear the names "Fannie Mae" and "Freddie Mac" bandied about all the time, either in newspaper stories or perhaps in a description of loan qualifications given you by your loan officer.

Likewise, an "FHA" loan or a "VA" loan doesn't mean that the FHA or the VA is actually making a loan to a home buyer or qualifying veteran. People don't go to the VA to get a home loan. They don't go to Fannie Mae, Freddie Mac, or the FHA either, for that matter. They go to lenders or brokers.

Fannie Mae is a nickname given to the Federal National Mortgage Association. Fannie Mae was formed in 1938 by the federal government for the sole purpose of fostering home ownership. In those days, and still today, "fostering home ownership" means providing liquidity in the mortgage marketplace. Freddie Mac, or the Federal Home Loan Mortgage Corporation, was formed in 1968, again by the federal government, to provide the very same function.

Neither Fannie Mae nor Freddie Mac makes loans; they establish lending guidelines so that lenders can buy loans from and sell them to one another as they see fit. Loans are now a commodity. They may vary in amount and be on different types of properties, such as a single unit, a duplex, a condominium, and so on. However, they're all the same; the only thing different about them is the names on the loans. Since loans are now a commodity, the only differentiating element is the price one pays for the loan.

Similarly, the Veterans Administration and the Department of Housing and Urban Development have the VA and FHA loan programs. They too establish guidelines for lenders to follow for the same reason: to provide liquidity when lenders need it.

Another aspect of VA and FHA loans is that if those loans go bad, the lender will get its money back. Should this happen, VA and FHA loans are "guaranteed" to the lender. As long as the lender making the original loan approved the loan using established government guidelines for these loans, if the loan goes into default, the lender is saved from the loan's going bad. However, if the VA loan was approved when it shouldn't have been and the VA points this out to the lender, the lender is stuck. The very same thing occurs under FHA rules; if an FHA loan goes into default through no fault of the original lender, the FHA will reimburse the lender for the outstanding loan balance.

CHAPTER 2

The Mortgage Loan Process

If you've never applied for a mortgage, just the application itself can be intimidating. This form, five pages long, has about 300 boxes that you're asked to put information into—all the while using words you've probably never used.

Mortgage companies make mortgages all day long—that's their job—so to the people in these companies, these terms are their second language, and they throw them around repeatedly, sometimes to each other and sometimes when they are talking to their customers.

Do you have to know all these terms? No, not at all. But there are definitely key words and processes that you absolutely must know about.

CONFIDENTIAL: Mortgage Calculators Found on the Internet Will Always Tell You to Buy

Are you ready to buy? Do you feel comfortable with the whole process? These are some emotional questions that you need to ask yourself before you go too much further. Regardless of what the advertisements say, not everyone needs a home mortgage just for the sake of having one. But if you pay attention, the message that you do is being pounded into your head at every turn. Or at least it seems that way when you begin thinking about owning your first home.

Sure, there are certain tax advantages to owning. Mortgage interest is one of the few tax deductions that is still around, so yes, there's certainly a tax advantage to owning your own home and taking out a home loan instead of paying rent. However, there are two types of issues you need to consider before you jump into the home-buying pool: financial and emotional.

From a financial perspective, there are significant tax advantages if you itemize your tax deductions. Not only will you have mortgage interest as a tax deduction, but you may also be able to deduct certain property taxes that you pay on the property.

You can run some of these numbers yourself by using one of the "rent versus buy" calculators found on pretty much any real estate or mortgage Web site. They're everywhere. I Googled the words "Rent + Buy + calculator" and got back over two million results. Such calculators use similar formulas, and they all take into consideration:

Current rent payment

Purchase price of home

Percentage down payment

Loan term

Rate

Years you plan on owning a home

Property taxes

Expected home appreciation

Your income tax bracket

Using these variables, the calculators attempt to determine whether or not—from a financial perspective, anyway—it makes sense for you to buy a house and take out a mortgage on it.

When you rent a property, you're not getting anything back on your monthly payments. You're giving someone else a part of your wealth in order to use that person's property. You get no property appreciation, you get none of the tax benefits, and there is no return on your monthly investment.

The odd thing about these calculators is they hardly ever tell you that it's not a good thing to buy a home. The numbers typically show that it's to the consumer's benefit to buy. There are many financial advantages to owning property, all of which are reflected in the criteria that these calculators use, so the calculators almost never tell you not to buy. The only time these things will tell you that it's not a good idea to buy is when rents in your area are ridiculously low and interest rates and the sale price of the home you're interested in are high. However, this situation would truly be an anomaly. If rates are high and homes are expensive, then you can expect rents to be high as well. These calculators will always tell you to buy.

CONFIDENTIAL: Knowing and Using the Following Terms Will Improve Your Chances of Not Being Taken Advantage Of

There is an exhaustive glossary at the back of this book, but there are certain key terms that you need to know and understand before you get involved in the mortgage process. These key terms are essential for two reasons:

1. Making certain that you're clear on what's happening during the critical points in your loan process

2. Letting those in the mortgage business know that you're an edu-
   cated consumer, so they shouldn't even try to mess with you

A few well-placed mortgage terms will help set the table when it
comes to finding a good lender who will listen to you and not fill your
mailbox with marketing pitches.

First and foremost, you're not making a loan application. Instead,
you're completing the 1003 (pronounced "ten-oh-three"). The 1003 is the
official form number that Fannie Mae has assigned to the five-page loan
application, and that's what everyone in the industry calls it.

You'll hear loan officers and loan processors talk to you about a loan
application, but behind closed doors, they call it the 1003. Every day. So
from this point forward, don't talk to a loan officer about completing a
loan application; ask him to send you a 1003 to fill out.

When you talk the lingo, you're giving notice that you've done your
homework and are wary of their little tricks.

Know the differences between loan prequalification, preapproval, approved with conditions, clear to close, and funded.

CONFIDENTIAL: A Prequalification Letter Is Essentially Worthless in Today's Real Estate Market.

A loan prequalification, or "prequal," means nothing more than that you
have had a discussion with a loan officer; you probably haven't even completed the 1003. A prequalification letter is a letter from your loan officer
stating that you and she have had a conversation and you've told her what
you do for a living, how much money you make, and what kind of bills
you have outstanding.

Based upon this conversation, a loan officer will type up a prequal
letter, essentially stating that based on what you told her and using standard loan qualification guidelines, you are hereby "prequalified" to buy a
house for a particular sales price and loan amount.

In the past, a potential home buyer would carry a prequalification letter around with him as he began shopping for a home. If a Realtor wanted to show homes to a home buyer, she would ask him if he had been prequalified. The consumer would answer yes, and the Realtor would then show him homes.

When a consumer found a home that he wanted to buy, the seller or the seller's Realtor would ask to see his prequalification letter. This would tell the seller that the potential buyer had spoken with a loan officer.

Few Realtors accept prequalification letters anymore when you make an offer. They prefer a preapproval letter to a prequalification letter

A preapproval letter takes the prequalification one step further. It isn't issued until the information provided to the loan officer has been verified and the credit report has been reviewed. Verification takes place using third-party sources. Income is verified by examining a recent paycheck stub, last year's W2 form, or both.

Having enough money to cover both the down payment and associated closing costs is verified by examining recent bank and investment statements showing that the buyer has enough money to close a particular deal based upon an assumed sales price.

A preapproval letter is issued only after review of the borrower's credit report. Most Realtors will accept a preapproval letter, but some want something even more solid: an approval letter with conditions.

CONFIDENTIAL: It's the Approval That Sellers Want to See

You'll notice right away there is no *pre* in front of the word *approval*. This means that not only has the 1003 been completed and verified, the credit report reviewed, and the existence of funds to close verified, but the loan has been reviewed either by an underwriter or by some type of automated underwriting system (AUS), and an approval has been issued, "subject to" certain conditions being met.

Common conditions would be things like providing enough insurance coverage to insure the home and making certain that all documents in the file (such as bank statements and paycheck stubs) aren't more than 90 days old.

This is the approval letter your Realtor wants to see—and so do the sellers of the property you want to buy.

The next stage is "clear to close." At this point, all conditions have been signed off on, everything is in order, the property has been evaluated, and your loan papers have been printed and are awaiting your signature. You won't ever have to worry about providing a clear to close letter to anyone, but your loan officer will tell you and your Realtor when you're at that stage.

And remember the old adage, "It ain't over 'til it's over." The last bit of approval comes when money changes hands. This stage is called *funding*. Your loan has funded when the home is officially yours. The keys are in your hand, and money has been electronically wired to the seller's bank account.

CONFIDENTIAL: Using Terms Used Only in the Lending Industry Will Put Your Loan Officer on Notice That You're Not to Be Messed Around With

If you know the words *1003, prequalification, preapproval, approved with conditions, clear to close,* and *funding,* you've nailed down the key words that you can drop with regularity, letting everyone involved know that not only are you not a dummy, but you're armed to the teeth with knowledge, and any attempts to pull the financial wool over your eyes will be met with more than just a typical "oh, that's okay" response.

Mortgage loan officers will treat you with kid gloves and won't try any of the tricks you'll read about in this book. They can't afford to; you speak their language.

It's also important that you know who the people in the loan process are. Some are important, and some are less so. But perhaps the three most important people you'll be dealing with while your loan is being approved are your loan officer, your loan processor, and the underwriter.

Your loan officer has one primary objective for her employer, regardless of whether she's working for a mortgage banker or a mortgage broker: to find new loans. She can find new loans in as many ways as in any other business, but primarily she gets referrals from Realtors, builders, and previous customers.

Another job your loan officer has is to take care of her borrowers after they apply for a loan. This can mean answering questions or helping with the approval process or providing input on which loan program to choose, but it's your loan officer who will be your contact in the early stages of loan application and loan approval.

A loan officer can go by many different titles, and its quite possible that you'll encounter several of them. A few business titles that a loan officer might go by include:

Loan Officer

Senior Loan Officer

Mortgage Consultant

Mortgage Loan Originator

Home Loan Consultant

Mortgage Planner

And as many other monikers as they can think up. Loan officers call themselves different things to differentiate them from other loan officers. But they all perform mostly the same duties: finding loans and guiding those loans through the approval process.

Your loan officer is the one who will help determine which loan is best for you, quote you mortgage rates and closing costs, and also be there if any problems arise throughout the approval process.

If you apply in person, you will apply for a loan with your loan officer, and if you apply online, you will be assigned one. He is the person who will collect your loan documentation, such as your pay stubs or insurance or tax returns. He is also the person who will issue the initial loan disclosures that are required by federal and state governments.

It's also possible that your loan officer will have an assistant (or two if she's one of the top loan officers in your area). Loan officers' assistants are the people who handle the daily issues of collecting the information from you that is needed to close your loan and screening out any questions they can handle that would interfere with your loan officer's primary objective of finding new loans for the company.

Loan officers who make $200,000 to $300,000 or more per year use assistants in one fashion or another. They have to; there's no way they could handle all their clients and still bring in new business without them.

While that's okay, understand that if you find this heavy-hitter loan officer whom you absolutely love and who does everything super-well, you just might be handed off to one of his assistants. That's not necessarily a really bad thing, as you'll probably be handed off only when your loan has the green light. It may be a problem, though; you may also find yourself handled by an assistant who doesn't have the mortgage skills that may be needed if and when problems arise.

But once your loan officer originates your loan, prequalifies or preapproves you, and sends you for processing, you'll be introduced to the next person in line—the loan processor.

CONFIDENTIAL: How Smooth Your Loan Closing Will Be Is Directly Proportional to How Long Your Loan Officer and Your Loan Processor Have Been Working Together

Loan processors are a loan officer's right hand. And left hand. Heck, good loan processors save more deals than their loan officer might know about. I've been originating loans for a long, long time, and I can tell you that behind every good loan officer is a damn good loan processor. Good loan officers can't be good loan officers without stellar loan-processing help.

Your loan processor documents your file by collecting the documentation required to get your loan approved and your loan papers drawn up. You'll probably spend more time with your loan processor than with your loan officer, especially if you've already decided on what type of loan you want.

That said, finding good loan processors is an ongoing process for top loan officers. If a loan processor has trouble closing the loan officer's loans, gets negative feedback from customers, and finds it hard to "spin plates" throughout the loan closing, then you can bet that the loan officer is out looking for new help.

Loan officers trust their loan processors with their income. I've personally closed more than 1,000 loans. I've worked with many loan processors through the years, and there are two that I would stake my loan life on. Their names are Teresa and Elizabeth.

If your loan officer and loan processor have been together for more than a couple of years, then you must realize that they've closed more than their fair share of loans. They know each other, they know how to handle files, and they communicate so well that each knows what the other is doing, without even asking.

As your loan moves closer and closer to closing, you'll be working more and more with your loan processor. If you find out how long your loan officer and your loan processor have been working together, you'll also find out how smooth your loan approval will be.

The last very important person in the loan process is the underwriter. You may never meet this person, or even know his name. The underwriter is the individual who establishes that everything you have provided in the form of documentation and loan qualification conforms to the appropriate lending guidelines.

Are you getting a Fannie Mae loan? Then it's the underwriter who makes sure that everything in the file that has been presented to him meets Fannie Mae guidelines. Whatever is needed for loan approval must be physically checked off by a person, and that person is your underwriter.

There are many more people involved in your loan, many that you'll never know about or hear from. But your loan officer, loan processor, and underwriter are the three towers when it comes to loan approval.

CONFIDENTIAL: Your Loan Isn't Approved by a Person or a Loan Committee Anymore

It used to be that after you submitted your loan application to your lender, a bunch of people sat around and reviewed your application and your income, looked at your credit report, and decided whether or not to approve your loan. This is not the way it works anymore. Your loan is now approved by a computer program, the automated underwriting system, or AUS.

The first AUS for home loans was developed in the mid-1990s by Fannie Mae and Freddie Mac. Fannie Mae's system is called the Desktop Underwriter (DU), and Freddie's version is called the Loan Prospector (LP). The FHA and the VA now have automated approvals as well, and even loans that don't fall into those categories can have their very own automated approval system.

This is where the "instant approval" and "apply now; answer in seconds" sort of marketing comes from. Most loans now are approved using this method.

These systems take the information you put on your loan application, pull a credit report along with your credit scores, and issue an approval. Or not. An AUS won't officially "decline" you if your loan application doesn't meet the guidelines, but it won't issue an approval. This may sound like nothing more than a quibble over terms, but it's actually a significant piece of the process.

There are a few loan programs and lending programs that still require a human underwriter to approve a mortgage application. In these in-

stances, you fill out an entire loan application and provide your loan officer with as much documentation as *you might need* in the course of a loan
approval.

On the few loan programs that still require a human underwriter,
you'll be asked to complete the entire loan application and to complete
every single bit of it as it pertains to you. This means listing every single
debt you might have, every bank account, every savings or retirement
account, your tax returns for the previous two years, all W2s—everything,
even if it's not going to be needed to approve your loan. The problem with
this is that some of the things you provide, voluntarily or because they
were asked for by your loan officer, can bring up other issues in your loan
application or simply delay the approval process because the additional
information that you provided to the lender must be verified by the underwriter.

The advantage of using an AUS is that you provide only what the
computer asks for *after* you submit your application. There are two basic
reasons for this advantage: borrower convenience and the possibility of
opening up a big ol' can of worms.

An AUS will take your loan application, either one completed by hand
or one done online, and assume that the information you put in all the
boxes is either correct or verifiable. If you say that you have $100,000 in
the bank, you make $5,000 per month, and you pay $1,200 per month in
child support, then the AUS will input those data, pull your credit scores,
and issue your approval. Or not.

CONFIDENTIAL: If You're Declined by an AUS, Your Loan Officer Can "Tweak" Your Application in an Attempt to Get Your Approval

What's tweaking? It's simply adjusting your application in order to receive
a favorable decision. Tweaking isn't lying. It's not making things up on
your application just to get an approval. Tweaking means adjusting certain elements on your application to get your approval.

Tweaking would never have been an option using the historical loan submission guidelines, where the loan application along with every bit of documentation would be collected, then sent to a human underwriter for an approval.

An underwriter looks at what is presented to her to see whether the loan conforms to the guidelines appropriate for that particular loan program. For instance, suppose you want a 15-year fixed-rate loan. Your loan officer and loan processor compile all the documentation needed to submit the loan.

An appraisal is completed; title work is done; tax returns, paycheck stubs, and bank statements are in the file. This documentation process can typically take two to three weeks. After everything is documented, the file is ultimately sent to the underwriter for an approval. If your loan officer has done his job right, there won't be any problems. But what if the 15-year loan that you want also pushes your debt ratios higher than the lending guidelines ask for?

Let's say the standard debt ratio for a 15-year fixed-rate loan is 33 percent with 5 percent down, and your debt ratio is 40 percent. A human underwriter may turn down the loan because of the high ratio. But what the underwriter won't do is rework the loan application to reflect a lower-payment, 30-year fixed-rate loan that would reduce your debt ratio.

That's not the underwriter's job. The underwriter makes sure that what is presented is within the guidelines established by the loan program you're trying to qualify for. If the underwriter declines your loan because of your high debt ratio, your entire file will be sent back to your loan officer.

You'll start all over, rework the file for a 30-year fixed-rate loan, and resubmit it. This can add several days to your loan approval. Perhaps the 30-year fixed-rate loan dropped your ratios only from 40 to 36, still higher than the program asks for. The underwriter could approve the loan based upon other strengths in the file, or again decline the loan and send it back to the loan officer.

Okay, what about an adjustable-rate mortgage to reduce the ratios further? Or maybe we borrow less? Maybe a co-borrower on the loan will help. Tweaking various parts of the loan application to get an approval the standard way would probably do nothing more than make the underwriter mad at your loan officer for continuously submitting a loan application that didn't fit the guidelines.

But with an AUS, changing loan scenarios can be done in a matter of minutes. Want to change to a 30-year fixed? No problem. Hey, what about a 40-year? Got a second? Let me check.

An AUS allows a loan officer to change part of the loan application, hit a key on the computer keyboard, and wait a few seconds—the typical time it takes for an AUS to reach a decision. Forget having to rework the file and resubmit it. The loan officer can make certain changes on the application and send the loan to the AUS for a decision.

When a loan officer gets an approval from an AUS, all the underwriter has to do is make sure that what you've provided in the file is what the AUS asked for. Does the AUS ask for three months of statements, and you provided them? Check. The two most recent pay stubs? Check.

Underwriters don't have to worry about debt ratios or assets in the bank. All the underwriter now does is verify that what is being asked for is present in the loan file. There is no declining and resubmitting. Instead, the loan officer finds the right loan using the AUS and fashions the application around that approval. This is totally opposite to how loans were approved as recently as the late 1990s.

When an AUS doesn't issue an approval, it lists the reasons why, in order of the significance of the issue. If the number one reason for the nonapproval is high debt ratios, the loan officer can find a lower rate, find a longer amortization period that lowers the payment, or lower the loan amount by putting more money down or buying a smaller house.

The loan officer then changes the application, pushes the "send" button, and waits for a few moments. No approval? Okay, let's change this. Still no approval? Okay, let's do this and do this. Approval? Yea! Now let's document the file based on how we changed the loan application and send it to the underwriter for sign-off.

Major tweaking will occur when the borrowers simply must borrow less, get a raise at work, or put more money down. If tweaking a loan application results in loan approval conditions that the borrower can't meet, then some decisions have to be made.

If you can't get your approval with your current income and you don't want to buy a smaller house, you simply need to wait until you get a raise or otherwise find more income. The neat thing about tweaking is that it gives borrowers a bona fide road map to get where they eventually want to be. Historically, it would be, "Hey, make a little more money or try to buy something in the $300,000 range and call me in six months."

With an AUS, it's more specific. "If you can get your income to $5,500 per month, get a 30-year fixed rate at 7.00 percent, and keep your credit where it is now or better, then we can do this deal."

CONFIDENTIAL: Some Lenders Won't Allow Tweaking

Your loan officer isn't required to resubmit your application to the AUS multiple times to get an approval. In fact, some loan officers aren't allowed to resubmit an application several times to try and obtain a loan approval.

Mortgage brokers, for example, may not have the ability to send a loan directly to a wholesale lender's AUS time and time again; instead, they might send it directly to Fannie Mae's or Freddie Mac's system. But these applications aren't free. They cost money, either to the broker or to the wholesale lender. The consumer won't pay for tweaking, but someone does.

The fee can vary, but an AUS decision might cost the loan officer $10 to $15 per decision. There are times when a loan may be resubmitted several times without additional charges, but in other situations, fees might be charged each time a decision is requested.

If you're working with a mortgage broker, you can bet that he won't be able to constantly resubmit your loan to the same online mortgage approval system in order to find an approval. If he did, you could expect a person from that bank to call your broker up and say, "Hey, what are you doing submitting this loan so many times? It's costing us money!" or something like that.

Don't expect your broker to resubmit too many times—maybe no more than a couple, especially if he has to pay money each time he resubmits your loan through an AUS. Instead, your broker will tell you, "We can't get an approval because you need to 'fill in the blank here.'" As long as you "fill in the blank here," you should get your approval.

Your loan could be tweaked more if you've already picked out a property and want to see if you can get an approval. That's when tweaking is most likely to occur. Your loan officer knows that you're serious. Instead of playing around with a series of "what if" scenarios, you actually have a property in mind.

If you haven't picked out a property, but you want your approval, then your loan officer will take basic information from you and work her way to an approval. She will ask you basic questions about your income, your job, and what kind of house you want to buy, then prequalify you based upon traditional loan parameters. If conventional ratios are 33/38, then your officer will take your gross monthly income, plug in some current mortgage rates, and work backward to find your approximate loan amount.

Automated underwriting systems also need two things in order to work: a property address and a sales price. This is a requirement for several reasons, but the most important one is to reserve the AUS for a loan decision on a bona fide deal, not to get someone preapproved for a loan. So what will your loan officer do? Fake the information in order to get a decision. When you get a real property, the fake address will be replaced by the property that you're buying.

Fake the information about the property, that is. Everything on your loan application that is pertinent to you—your credit, your job, and your assets—is real, but your loan officer will use something like

123 Main Street
MyTown, USA

Along with an approximate sales price and estimated down payment. After your loan officer enters these fake data, she will upload your application to the AUS, wait a few seconds, then "Voila! Instant loan approval." But if your loan officer is restricted from making multiple submissions, then you may have to flat out ask her to resubmit if you don't get the desired result.

Finally, when you get an accepted contract on a real property, the loan officer simply opens up your application and resubmits it with the real property address, sales price, and down payment.

In my experience, I had the ability to resubmit a loan up to 15 times before I was charged again for an AUS. I could do this because (1) I was an experienced loan officer and (2) I was a mortgage banker and didn't have to submit the application to another lender to get a decision.

Tweaking works only when you're t-h-i-s close to getting your approval. Maybe your debt ratios might need to be reworked from 49 to 44. Tweaking doesn't mean that a loan officer has no clue as to where or how to approve your deal. It means that your loan officer knows that your loan application is "approvable" but not quite there.

CONFIDENTIAL: An Experienced Loan Officer Will Know When to Tweak and When Not To

What things give loan officers the idea that while your initial loan request wasn't approved, your loan is approvable? Experience and the ability to look at your loan to see what makes it a candidate for tweaking.

For instance, I had a client who bought investment properties on occasion, about two per year. The first couple of properties he bought went without a hitch. But the third home he purchased gave me some initial heartburn.

On the third deal, his ratios were much higher, not because rates had gone up, but because his debt ratios had; he had just added two new mortgages to his portfolio, and his total debt ratios were approaching 50 percent. That's high.

I didn't get my loan approval on the first try. It surprised me a little, because this guy was "golden" in terms of loan qualification. Yeah, his ratios were high, but his credit was spotless, with a score of over 800, and he had lots of money lying around in the bank—so much money that if push came to shove, he could write a check for the whole thing, but hey, that's what a mortgage is for, right?

He wanted a 15-year rate and didn't get it. I suggested that he either negotiate the price a bit lower, put more money down, or a combination of both. He attempted to lower the price, but he wasn't successful.

I resubmitted the loan on a 20-year fixed rate under the exact same scenario, except that this time I dropped the sales price from $600,000 to $590,000. His ratios dropped to 47. I resubmitted the loan to the AUS and got my approval. I called my client and told him that I had just gotten his approval, but on different terms. If he could get the seller to reduce the price to $590,000, still make a 20 percent down payment, and use a 20-year fixed rate instead of a 15, I could issue an approval letter right there on the spot.

I supplied my client with his approval letter under the approval terms using the new information. My client made the new offer, this time with his approval letter in hand. The seller accepted. But it's possible that my client would have lost the deal without an approval letter issued under those specific terms.

If my client's ratios had originally been 70 but needed to be 40, I would not have tweaked him. There would have been no need to, as there would be no reason to even try with such a disparity.

To clear the loan application for closing, all I had to do was read down the list of required items issued by the automated approval.

The AUS allows you to do some streamlining. The only things you need to put on your loan application are the things required to issue your approval.

CONFIDENTIAL: You Don't Have to Supply Tons of Documentation at Application, Even if Your Loan Officer Asks for It

You may still see loan officers who ask for absolutely everything up front, perhaps even before you have picked out a property. This is old school. Not a bad thing, mind you, but still old school.

There's no reason to start digging out all your old financial statements, tax returns, divorce decree, whatever—unless the AUS asks for it. Unfortunately, there are too many loan officers who ask for absolutely everything that could possibly be required for a mortgage approval at the very beginning of the loan process.

It's a real pain to drag out all sorts of documentation if it's not needed. The catch with such an approach is that whatever you provide, your lender has to verify. If you say you have $12,298 in a savings account, $49,442,235 in lottery winnings reserved for your grandkids, and about 14 other investment accounts worth about $13,988, then guess what? Your lender will have to verify every single item you entered on the application—whether or not you need that information to close the deal.

I'll give you an example.

You want to buy a $200,000 house, put 5 percent down, and have the seller pay for all your closing costs. You need, approximately, 5 percent of $200,000, or $10,000. So you provide three months' bank statements showing $12,533 in your account. So far, so good. You're done, right?

But you also put down that you have a 401(k) account, an IRA with about $9,500 in it, and an investment account with another $5,000. Since you put all that information on your application, your lender has to verify it, whether or not you needed it to close your deal.

You may have needed only $10,000 to close the $200,000 purchase, but since you added all that other stuff, you have to provide documentation proving your claims. This means more documentation and more work on your part.

And each time you provide more information, there's the possibility of more problems—problems that may not necessarily lead to your loan being declined, but that will cause you more headaches.

CONFIDENTIAL: Giving More Information Means You Have to Document More

Let's say that, because you want to make your application look as good as possible, you entered every piece of financial information about yourself. So one of the bank accounts you put on your 1003 shows a balance of $20,000, with a deposit of $15,000 made a few weeks ago. But you didn't need the $15,000 to buy your new home.

Sudden increases in deposit amounts attract the scrutiny of underwriters. Where did that money come from? Is it a loan? Is there another business or job that we don't know about? If it's a loan, do you have to pay it back? If you do, then your debt ratios would be affected. Did you get a gift from someone? Did you transfer funds from one account to another? If so, why, and were those accounts yours or were they accounts of others?

Prove it.

It's not your underwriters' fault. It's their job. Whatever you put on your loan application, they have to verify it. If you don't need it, don't put it on the application. It saves you time, and it saves them time.

If you have a loan officer who immediately, upon application, asks for all your stuff, simply ask, "Why are you asking me for all of this stuff now?"

Instead, you need to work with your loan officer to determine how much money, or "cash to close," will be required to close your deal. Whatever is needed, you simply supply that. Nothing more, nothing less.

CONFIDENTIAL: Some Things on Your Loan Application Are Completely Unnecessary

Your 1003 is five pages long, with more boxes than you can count, and your loan officer is asking you to fill out the application. "Which part?" you ask. "Why, all of it," replies your loan officer.

Here are some things you can mostly ignore on your loan application.

First and foremost, if you have no clue as to what the application is asking for, don't feel compelled to complete that information or frantically track down your loan officer to ask what you should put down. If you're scratching your head wondering what in the world you should put down, then leave it blank. If it's vital, your loan officer will help you fill in the blanks.

First, lenders don't care if you don't know what type of loan you want. At the very top of page 1, your 1003 asks you what kind of loan you're looking for. Heck, most people don't know that. So leave it blank if you feel like it.

Another section on the first page of the 1003 asks how many years of school you've had. As if that matters. It doesn't. I've seen loan applicants who, perhaps embarrassed, put "eight" or "ten" years of school. I imagined how stressed out they were, thinking that how much education they had would affect their loan approval. So maybe they fudged a little bit and put down that they graduated from high school or got their G.E.D. and were worrying that somehow the lender would find out that they lied about that and they would be declined.

It doesn't matter. If you've had 20 years of college, put that down. If you dropped out in the third grade, put that down. It just doesn't matter. Years of education is an old, bogus box. A college graduate is no more deserving of a home loan than someone who dropped out of high school to help her parents make ends meet.

Page 2 of the 1003 can sometimes be very intimidating, especially to those who are buying their first home. There are no less than nine sections that ask you to list all of your checking, savings, and retirement accounts.

It's intimidating because, human nature being what it is, if there's a blank spot, people think, "I'd better fill it in."

Don't worry about any of that. Just complete what you need to do the deal. Don't feel that you need to have 18 different investment accounts, some mutual funds, and stock accounts lying around in your sofa cushions. Lenders don't care about everything you have; they just care about whether you have enough to close the loan.

If you look further down on page 2, you'll see a section asking you to list your automobiles. And any jewelry or furniture. Tell the loan application to take a hike. This again is an old school loan question that's not needed and, in my opinion, is kind of embarrassing to ask.

If you take a loan application at a lender's office and your loan officer asks you if you have a car and, if so, what kind is it and what is it worth, then I suggest you walk away and fine another loan officer.

"Pardon me, can you now tell me what jewelry you own?" What is this, a pawnshop? Give me a break.

If your loan officer takes you through these questions, then you also know that he's not at all well versed in the loan approval process. He's simply an application taker, and if there's a problem with your loan application, he won't know how to deal with it. And you're the one who will get screwed. The loan officer goes back to work the next day. You may have lost the house you wanted to buy.

So where do these questions come from? They've been around for a long time. A very long time. The furniture and jewelry question is an old "net worth" question that grumpy bankers would use to evaluate your loan application.

So, too, was the automobile question placed in the mix. Your car is an asset—at least, it will be when you pay it off and retire the note so that it is fully yours. The automobile question also added something else to the underwriting matrix: If you didn't put down a car on your application, the underwriter would want to know how you got to work.

Honestly, this has happened to me, and to most loan officers who've been in the business for several years. If there was no car listed as an asset, the underwriter would want to know how the applicant got to work. Why?

If the borrower had a job, she had to get there, right? And if she had a car, she probably had a car payment. If she had a car payment, that would affect her debt ratios and perhaps her ability to qualify for a mortgage loan.

To add to the insult, the application asks how old the car is. If the car is just a couple of years old, the underwriter would suspect that there was a car payment somewhere that wasn't showing up on the credit report. In this case, the underwriter would demand, and get, a copy of a clear title to the car to prove that no car payment was being made.

I'm not kidding about all of this. But the 1003 still asks for stuff that's not needed. And it can be intimidating to think that just because there are boxes to fill doesn't mean that you have to fill them.

Automated underwriting has eliminated most of the fluff, yet the loan application still asks for it.

CONFIDENTIAL: Some Boxes Are Simply for Identification and Won't Be Used to Determine Eligibility

Another entry on page 1 of the 1003 asks for your age. This box isn't needed to determine whether or not you're young enough to take out a 30-year loan.

"Yeah, this guy wants a 30-year mortgage, but he's already 65, so we should probably turn him down because he'll never last long enough to pay off the loan," says an imaginary lender.

I have been asked this question on more than one occasion. Once it was by a daughter who was helping to fill out a loan application for her aging father. She actually said, "Would they approve him for a 30-year loan if he's that old? He surely won't live that long." First, this is age discrimination. Lenders can't deny a loan based upon age.

Okay, if someone is too young to enter into a legally binding contract, then yes, no loan will be approved. But if my 92-year-old grandmother applied for a 30-year mortgage and the bank said, "No, we can't approve you for a 30-year loan, but we can lend you some money based upon a 2-year loan because that's how long we think you're going to live," then you can bet that I and my army of lawyers wouldn't stop suing the bank for age discrimination.

The "Age" box is used to help determine identity, not to decide whether or not to make a loan based upon how old or how young a person is.

C H A P T E R   3

Risk Elements

Before I get into the confidential information, first I have to explain the risk factors that lenders evaluate when looking at your loan.

Risk elements in loan underwriting are those items that assess these questions:

1. Can you pay us back?
2. Will you pay us back?
3. What if you don't?

Can You Pay Back the Lender?

This question evaluates whether you have the financial wherewithal to pay back the money you've borrowed to buy the home. This means that you have enough money to make the house payment, while also paying for your daughters' braces, the car, the gasoline, the cell phone bill, the dinners out, the dinners in . . . well, do you have enough money to do everything you have the responsibility to do, while at the same time enjoying life?

Traditionally, this ability to pay the lender back on time every month was determined by a *debt ratio*.

A debt ratio is a lending term that expresses, as a percent, your monthly bills divided by your gross monthly income. Debt ratios are part of a risk element, and there are two ratios. The first ratio is sometimes called the housing ratio or "front" ratio, and the second ratio is called the total, "back," or "back end" debt ratio. A front debt ratio is arrived at by dividing your house payment by your gross monthly income. For example, suppose you have a house payment of $1,500 and a gross monthly income of $5,000. $1,500 ÷ $5,000 = 0.30, or 30 percent. Your front, or housing, ratio is 30.

Now add all your other debts beyond housing, not including items that won't appear on a credit report, such as your electric bill, food, or going out to the movies. Other debt includes minimum credit card payments, automobile loans, and other obligations, secured or nonsecured, that you borrowed and are expected to pay back. Other debt may also include child-support or spousal payments.

If your car payment is $400, your credit card payments add up to $300, and your student loans make up another $200, then you would add those sums to your housing payment of $1,500 to arrive at $2,400.

Divide $2,400 by $5,000 per month gross monthly income and your back ratio is 48. Your ratios are 30/48.

Will You Pay Back the Lender?

You may have the money to pay the lender back, but will you? This is determined by your credit past. Have you borrowed money from other companies, yet didn't pay them back? This is the element of risk that helps determine not your ability to pay, as represented by your debt ratios, but whether or not you have the inclination to pay back the original lender at all.

I have seen more than my share of loan applications where the borrower made tons of money, but, for whatever reason, was simply late on his mortgage payments. He had the capacity to pay back the loan, but he didn't have the credit responsibility to carry out that obligation.

What if You Don't Pay Back the Lender?

This risk element is the element of last resort. If the borrower doesn't pay back the loan, will the lender get its money back if it is forced to take the house and sell it to someone else?

The third risk element is not the borrower, but the physical collateral. If the home goes into foreclosure, can the lender sell the property and get its money back? Lenders don't like foreclosures. They hate them with a passion. It means that they screwed up in the first place and have to make up for it.

In case those bad things do happen, the lender needs to know a little more about its physical asset—the house itself. This is provided by an appraisal, an independent report that examines recent home sales near the subject property that can support the value.

Is the house located in a neighborhood dominated by homes made of brick, but the loan is being made on a home made of straw? Or mud? Is the subject property a 1,200-square-foot two-bedroom, one-bath home located in a subdivision dominated by four-bedroom, three-bath properties? In other words, is the house like everyone else's? If it is, the lender increases its chances of selling the home quickly should a foreclosure be necessary.

Okay, all that having being said, let's go on.

CONFIDENTIAL: Mortgage Lenders Can Adjust Risk Elements 1 and 2, but They Can't Adjust Element 3

You can find your perfect dream home, but if it doesn't fit the plan, it's not going to work. If your debt ratios are well within lending guidelines and you have great credit, but your property isn't quite right with the rest of the neighborhood, you're going to have major problems that even your excellent credit with no nonpayments can't overcome.

Lenders don't like to make loans on odd eggs. Loans are made based upon both the individual and the property. Both have to work. If one doesn't, the deal's dead.

Lenders evaluate properties based upon the appraisal. A typical property appraisal will examine the subject property, then look at a minimum of three other similar properties in the area to see if they "match."

If a borrower buys a house in a subdivision, chances are that the builder has built homes that are similar in design. A builder will typically construct "like" properties, then add some upscale ones later on down the road. Or maybe she'll build some upscale ones first, then less so later on. In other words, there will be a good mix of houses, yet they won't be too different from one another in terms of design and utility. Builders know that if they get too eccentric with their properties, buyers may have a hard time finding financing.

Lending requirements demand that the appraisal identify similar properties in the neighborhood—a minimum of three—that have sold within the previous 12 months. Sound tough? Well, it really should be. Lenders don't want their houses back. They're not in the real estate business. They're in the lending business. Unlike Realtors, when lenders sell property, it usually means that they're losing their tails. When Realtors sell property, they're making money.

CONFIDENTIAL: If the Property Doesn't Conform to Specific Appraisal Guidelines, You Won't Be Able to Get a Loan

Over the years, I've gotten lending requests for some fairly unusual situations. I recall a property in southern California where the owners went a tad overboard in renovating their home. Originally, the home was built as a three-bedroom house, just like most of the homes in the area.

But in the early 1990s, the new owners gutted much of the house and redesigned it to fit their own "style." They got rid of two of the bedrooms and made a huge library and reading room with a fireplace. Sounds nice so far, right?

In the main room, they wanted to expand the fireplace that was currently there by adding imported Italian marble. This cost them a fortune, but it was their taste. The updated fireplace alone was massive and had a price tag close to $50,000—in a house that probably would sell for $300,000.

Soon, they decided to sell their masterpiece. Who wouldn't buy this house, right? After all, it had a huge library with a fireplace and a main fireplace in the main room that was almost as big as the room itself. The fireplace, remember, was made of imported Italian marble. They listed their home, and couldn't wait to make a fortune off of their remodeling.

But it didn't sell. It seems that no one wanted a one-bedroom home with a huge library. And the Italian marble fireplace looked sort of, well, discothèque. The house was on the market forever, or so it seemed. It was even listed by Realtors as a "one of a kind one-bedroom." Who in the world would buy a one-bedroom home in a three-bedroom neighborhood?

Okay, maybe you found someone, but would he be enamored with the Italian marble as well?

Guess what, they found a buyer. The buyer came to me for a loan. The buyer had a great job, great credit, and a good down payment. But I couldn't get a loan for him. There were no similar sales in the area. Forget the Italian marble stuff; there were no other one-bedroom homes in the market or anywhere close by. Lenders would not make a loan on that property.

Lenders can make exceptions with debt ratios and adjust for credit issues, but they typically can't get past property problems.

CONFIDENTIAL: Lenders Can Eliminate the Need for a Down Payment

It seems that almost everyone thinks that you need a down payment to buy a home. Wrong. Lenders don't need a down payment, but they do need to make adjustments when and if you decide not to make one or otherwise don't have the ability to put your hard-earned cash into the equation when you decide to buy.

No-money-down loans aren't a secret, but for some reason they're made out to be so. Perhaps it's simply the public's perception that down payment money is a requirement.

But nothing could be further from the truth. Every lender that I know of offers a competitive zero-down loan program. In fact, most lenders offer a variety of zero-down loans in two basic varieties:

No money down at all

Money down, but it's not yours

CONFIDENTIAL: Zero-Down Loans Can Be a Trap

Zero-down loans are just that. In some cases, they come in an 80/20 form, where there are two loans on one property, one for 80 percent of the value of the home and one for 20 percent, effectively eliminating any need for a down payment whatsoever. Zero-down loans can also come in a straight 100 percent fashion.

So why doesn't everyone take a zero-down loan? For one thing, the interest rates are higher than for mortgages with a down payment involved. In fact, they're much higher. A zero-down 100 percent loan could be at 7.50 percent, while a mortgage of a similar term with a down payment could be as low as 6.00 percent. When they eliminate the down payment, lenders offset that increased risk with more interest.

Another reason not to take a zero-down loan is that it can be a risky move unless you're certain that you're never going to sell that house, or at a minimum will not move for a long while. Why? Because if you ever have to sell the property, you'll have closing costs.

When sellers sell, they typically do so by paying off all associated loan costs with the proceeds of the sale.

For instance, a home is for sale for $500,000 and has a mortgage balance on it of $150,000. The seller bought the home several years ago, and because of regular loan amortization and property appreciation, there's plenty of equity in the deal. Selling costs could be as high as $40,000. At the settlement table:

Sales price	$500,000
Payoff	$ 150,000
Less closing costs	$ 40,000
Net to seller	$ 310,000

Now let's review a home with no money down and someone who has to sell within a couple of years. A buyer buys a house for $500,000 with no money down. The interest rate is 7.50 percent amortized over 30 years. The monthly payment would be $3,497.

After a year, the buyer gets a new job in another state and must move, so she sells the house. With natural loan amortization, the loan balance after the first year is $495,390. There's also been some appreciation, so she sells at $510,000. At the settlement table:

Sales price	$510,000
Payoff	$495,390
Less Closing Costs	$ 40,000
Net to seller	($25,390)

The seller has to either bring a check in the amount of $25,390 to the closing table or not sell and wait until the loan balance goes down some more, home prices rise, or a combination of both.

Zero-down loans can be a trap. If you have no down payment funds available, then this is something you need to look at, just to understand your options, or at least the lack thereof. Your lender couldn't care less whether you take a zero-down loan or one with a down payment. It doesn't matter to the lender one way or another.

CONFIDENTIAL: Alternative Sources for Down Payment Money Are Better than Zero-Down Loans

Another way to get into a house with no money down is by letting someone else give you the money to do so. That's not a bad deal if you can swing it, right? Down payment money can come in the form of a gift, a grant, or a forgivable loan.

The FHA allows a family member, a nonprofit organization, or your trade union to give you the money you need to buy a home. Usually this is about 3 percent of the sales price and an additional amount for closing costs.

There are other allowances for down payment assistance that can be designed by local, county, or state governments for teachers, veterans, firefighters, cops, and other public servants.

Lenders don't have a problem with such loan programs, as long as the loan program is specifically designed to accept such gifts and grants and follows the various rules and requirements that guide them. Your buddy at work can't give you a gift to buy a home using an FHA loan. Neither can the girls at the book club. These gifts must come from approved sources.

Your gift can't look like it's a loan. A loan would mean that you'd have to pay it back, affecting your debt ratios, and it's possible that the gift giver would want an interest in the property in some fashion.

CONFIDENTIAL: It's Okay if You Don't Have a Down Payment—but It Will Affect Your Monthly Payments

If you have no money to close on a home, that's okay. Really it is. For some reason, consumers think that down payments are a requirement or that if you don't have a down payment, then your home loan is coming from a band of loan sharks.

But let's get a little background first on why this mortgage down payment myth is so pervasive.

A few decades ago, down payments were a requirement. But back in 1934, the Federal Housing Agency was created to help foster home ownership. The country had just suffered through the Great Depression, and what better way to get the country going again than to put as many people as possible into their very own homes?

One of the biggest obstacles when buying a home was having enough money for a down payment. In those days, mortgages were indeed made from other people's deposits, and banks could establish any lending policy they saw fit.

To protect their depositors' assets, the banks would require a hefty down payment. But with the FHA, lenders could make a mortgage loan with as little as 3 percent down, and if the loan ever went bad, the lender could get its money back from this government program as long as the loan was made in accordance with FHA lending rules.

In 1957, an insurance company came up with a better idea. Instead of requiring that home buyers put up a minimum of 20 percent down to buy a home, the insurance company came up with a policy that said, "Okay, if your borrower defaults on the loan, we'll make up the difference in the down payment"—in other words, mortgage insurance.

This is not to be confused with an insurance policy that pays off a home loan in the event of the borrower's death. It's a policy that pays the lender the difference between 20 percent down and what the buyer actually put down.

The borrower puts less than 20 percent down, say 10 or 5 percent or even nothing, and the borrower buys an insurance policy that covers the difference between the 80 percent level and actual down payment.

CONFIDENTIAL: Beware of Lenders Who Say, "I Figured Out a Way That You Don't Have to Pay Mortgage Insurance"

Mortgage insurance is a policy that is paid for by the borrower, with the benefits going to the lender. Is this a fair shake? Of course it is; the buyer didn't have to come up with a full 20 percent down payment; he got to put as little as zero down.

Mortgage insurance premiums can vary depending upon the loan type (fixed or adjustable) and the amount of risk the policy is covering. The more down payment, the less risk; hence, the lower the premium.

A good way to estimate how much mortgage insurance costs is to multiply the loan amount by $1/2$ percent, then divide by 12 to get the monthly premium. Just as with most other insurance policies, the buyer can pay monthly or pay a single premium. Let's look at some sample monthly payments with mortgage insurance attached.

Sales price	$300,000	$300,000	$300,000
Down payment	10%	5%	0%
Loan amount	$270,000	$285,000	$300,000
30-year fixed rate	6.50%	6.50%	7.00%
Mortgage insurance	0.50%	0.70%	1.00%
Loan payment	$ 1,706	$ 1,801	$ 1,995
MI payment	$ 112	$ 166	$ 250
Total payment	$ 1,818	$ 1,967	$ 2,245

You'll notice that as the down payment decreases, the mortgage insurance premium increases. In the last column, with 0 percent down, not only does the mortgage insurance premium rise significantly, but so does the interest rate. Since a key risk element, the down payment, is affected, it is offset by a higher mortgage rate. Yes, the monthly payments are higher with zero down, but you didn't have to use any of your money to buy the house.

One drawback of mortgage insurance is that, at least as of this writing, since it is not mortgage interest, it's not a tax-deductible item. The mortgage insurance industry has tried for years to make its case to the legislature to allow mortgage insurance to be tax-deductible, but so far its efforts haven't paid off.

Since mortgage insurance is required for all first-mortgage loans above 80 percent of the value of the home, then why not take out two loans? That makes sense, right? If you put 5 percent down, and you have a loan amount secured at 80 percent of the sales price, then you either need to get a mortgage insurance policy to cover the remaining 15 percent or find another mortgage, called a "second" mortgage. This structure is called an 80-15-5.

Another common structure involving a second mortgage has 10 percent down and a 10 percent second mortgage, called an 80-10-10. Still another arrangement is called an 80/20, with no money down and a second mortgage representing 20 percent of the sales price. Let's now look at how subordinate financing works compared with a mortgage loan that carries a mortgage insurance premium.

Sales price	$300,000	$300,000	$300,000
Down payment	10%	5%	0%
Loan amount	$240,000	$240,000	$240,000
Second loan amount	$ 30,000	$ 45,000	$ 60,000
30-year fixed rate (first)	6.50%	6.50%	7.00%
Second loan rate	8.50%	9.00%	10.00%
Loan payment 1	$ 1,516	$ 1,516	$ 1,596
Loan payment 2	$ 230	$ 362	$ 526
Total payment	$ 1,746	$ 1,878	$ 2,122

Notice something? These total monthly payments are remarkably similar to the payments with mortgage insurance. In this example, both loans were amortized over 30 years and were at fixed rates, but there are countless compositions that could include a 15-year fixed rate, adjustable, or other combinations.

The loan officer will run some numbers comparing your options when you have less than 20 percent down and show you a chart similar to this one, to show how smart she is by devising a secret plan to let you put less than 20 percent down without having to buy mortgage insurance.

"I have less than 20 percent down; do I have to have mortgage insurance?" you ask.

"Why, I have an idea that will let you get into your dream home with only 5 percent down and avoid mortgage insurance altogether! Remember, mortgage insurance isn't tax deductible, but mortgage interest is!" proclaims your loan officer.

Big deal. Every lender can offer this program, and quite frankly, your lender doesn't care if you take this or mortgage insurance; it's no skin off her nose. But loan officers and mortgage marketing materials make mortgage insurance out to be some kind of plague, and it's not.

CONFIDENTIAL: There May Be a Better Option Than Subordinate Financing, and It Involves Mortgage Insurance

One of the better options for those with less than 20 percent down involves a mortgage insurance premium with no subordinate financing. In fact, the mortgage insurance becomes tax-deductible. It's called a financed mortgage insurance premium.

In this type of policy (which is little known, by the way, but every lender who offers mortgage insurance also has this in its arsenal), the mortgage insurance is rolled into the original loan balance. The policy works only when you have 10 percent down, but it can work out better than an 80-10-10 structure.

On a $300,000 home with 10 percent down, the loan comes to $270,000. You also acquire a mortgage insurance premium that isn't made monthly; instead, the entire premium is rolled into the loan amount.

Using the very same figures as in the previous example, the mortgage insurance premium would be about 2.75 percent of the original loan, which would then be rolled into the original loan amount of $270,000. The new loan amount would be $277,425.

The monthly payment based upon 6.50 percent and 30 years is $1,753, very close to the $1,746 for an 80-10-10. Yet there is no mortgage insurance payment; it's rolled into the loan. Yes, you're adding the amount of the mortgage insurance premium to the principal, and yes, it puts a dent into your original equity.

The neat thing about this mortgage insurance premium is that it's refundable when you refinance later on down the road, although the amount you get back is lower the longer you wait to refinance. In this example, after 60 months, you would get about $3,000 back from your original premium, and if you refinanced three years after the original loan, you'd get more than half of that premium back—a little over $4,000 in mortgage insurance refund.

The point is not to think that there is an "either/or" choice when it comes to mortgage insurance or subordinate financing. It's just that because your loan officer rarely uses a financed premium (or has even heard of it, for that matter), you probably won't be given that option.

I used this very program to buy a house in Austin, Texas, and it was hands-down the best choice. I had 10 percent that I wanted to put down on a home. I financed my mortgage insurance premium, the payments were lower than any subordinate financing available at the time, and I refinanced a couple of years later and got a mortgage insurance refund.

CONFIDENTIAL: The Higher Rates Go, the More Attractive Mortgage Insurance Becomes

Mortgage rates are set by the credit markets. But mortgage insurance premiums can stay the same, even when rates are moving up. The mortgage insurance multiplier remains constant, meaning that while rising mortgage rates can increase your monthly payments, the mortgage insurance premium will stay the same.

Compare a $300,000 home with 10 percent down using different rates:

30-year first mortgage	6.00%	$240,000	$1,436
15-year second mortgage	8.50%	$ 30,000	$ 289
Total payment	$1,725		
30-year first mortgage	8.50%	$240,000	$1,844
15-year second mortgage	11.00%	$ 30,000	$ 336
Total payment	$2,180		

Now look at that same scenario with 10 percent down and a mortgage insurance payment:

30-year first mortgage	6.00%	$270,000	$1,616
Mortgage insurance premium	$ 112		
Total payment	$ 1,728		
30-year first mortgage	8.50%	$270,000	$1,886
Mortgage insurance premium	$ 112		
Total payment	$1,998		

When rates are relatively low, the total monthly payments are remarkably similar: $1,725 versus $1,728, for example. But as rates increase, the 10 percent down with mortgage insurance is much lower: $1,998 compared to $2,180.

CONFIDENTIAL: Down Payments Will Come Under Strict Scrutiny—and the Less Down Payment You Have, the More Scrutiny You Will Receive

If you are like most people and are inclined to put some money into a home in the form of a down payment, lenders care where you get it from. As mentioned earlier, it has to be yours. At least, it has to be yours in the form of a gift or a grant. There are some acceptable sources for down payments and some that are not acceptable.

Acceptable

Your savings account

Your checking account

Any publicly traded stocks you own

Bonds

Mutual funds

Equity in other property

Retirement accounts, including 401(k)s and IRAs

Sale of appraisable assets

Savings and checking accounts are easily verifiable. You'll only need to provide three months' most recent bank statements. Why three? Good question, but three statements will typically be enough to show your regular income along with regular deposits. It shows you putting your paycheck into the bank twice per month or transferring monies to a savings account.

Publicly traded stocks can be used. Some loan programs require that you not only prove ownership of the stocks by showing a minimum of three months' ownership, but also cash those stocks in and deposit the proceeds in your bank account. Most programs have shied away from this requirement and simply want to verify that you own those stocks, they're yours, and it's safe to assume that's where your money is coming from.

Several years ago, conventional lending required that you cash in the stocks, deposit the proceeds, and provide a copy of the deposit receipt. Now however, verification of ownership along with an acceptable valuation of the stock being used is acceptable.

Of course, bonds or mutual funds are treated in much the same way. You'll need to show that you have access to bond funds. Have those bonds matured, or what is the current value of those funds should you decide to tap into them? Mutual funds will also be verified by three months' most recent statements.

Equity in other property means that you sold another house to buy a new one. In this case, be prepared to not only provide bank statements, but also have a copy of the signed settlement statement from your previous sale.

Most retirement funds allow owners to borrow from those funds or use them to buy a home. Verification of ownership and the terms and conditions for how those funds may be accessed to buy a home will have to be reviewed by an underwriter.

CONFIDENTIAL: Anything That Can Be Appraised Can Be Used as Down Payment Funds

Your baseball card collection? Your Rolex watch? Your car? Anything that can be professionally appraised can be a legitimate source of funds to close a real estate deal. What is a "professional" appraisal? If you can get an insurance policy on it, it's probably appraisable.

I've got a baseball card collection. I've got a couple of Mickey Mantle rookie cards, a Jackie Robinson card, a Frank Robinson rookie—okay, don't get me started. But these are all appraisable assets. No, I won't go to closing with my Roberto Clemente Topps in hand, but if I wanted to use those cards as funds to buy real estate, then I could.

Because baseball cards can be professionally appraised, they can be a source of funds. "Hey, Dave, how'd you get that nice new house?" "Two Mickey Mantle Bowman rookies!"

I would have to show ownership of those cards by taking them to a professional appraiser, who would verify that I've got them and provide a written estimate of their worth. I would then have to sell those cards, either to an individual or to a card dealer, and verify the transaction.

Nice watch? Is it appraisable? Sell it. Car? Sell it and document it. If you can get an appraisal on it, it can be used.

CONFIDENTIAL: There Are Several Unacceptable Sources of Down Payment Funds

Cash on hand

Borrowed funds that are unsecured

Sweat equity

Almost anything that can't be proven to be yours

Cash on hand needs to have some history. It needs to have a source. Lenders aren't trying to make you out to be a drug dealer or a bookie; they're trying to ascertain that there aren't other loans against the property that they may not know about. If you've got a few thousand dollars lying around, be prepared to explain how you got it.

Often, a simple response of "I don't trust banks, so I keep my money at home in a safe" is sufficient. In the lending industry, such funds are called "mattress money"; the moniker works because it's assumed that the borrower stashes a 20-dollar bill under the mattress every Friday.

Lenders understand certain cultural differences when it comes to mattress money if you can account for it. The lender won't let you come to the closing table with a bunch of rolled-up ten-dollar bills; it will ask that you put it in a deposit account or obtain a cashier's check.

If you use the "I don't trust banks" reason to have a wad of cash in your hand, but at the same time you have an ATM card and a checking account, you can bet that your mattress money account explanation will be shot full of holes.

You can't borrow money from credit cards or other nonsecured sources. You can borrow against other real estate, but you just can't put your down payment on a credit card.

Sweat equity is a loose term that means that all the work you person-ally did on a property would have cost so many thousands of dollars if the lender had gone out and hired someone to do it. If you wanted to buy a home that needed a new roof and a new bathroom, and you volunteered to do all the work yourself without the lender's having to pay you, that would be sweat equity.

Sweat equity is too difficult to assign value to, much less keep track of the work you've done. Don't count on sweat equity as a source of funds to close.

The final caveat on unacceptable sources of funds: Just about any-thing that you can't prove is yours, the lender won't count. Sound unfair? Maybe, but down payments are a risk element that lenders use to deter-mine loan approval, and hey, if it's their money, you have to play by their rules.

C H A P T E R   4

Closing Costs

If you haven't guessed already, there are closing costs when you buy a home. There are lots of them, many with names that you've never even heard of. There are definite ways to save on closing costs, however. Some of those ways even your lender will tell you about. Others you have to ask for.

CONFIDENTIAL: Recurring Closing Costs Are Nonnegotiable; Nonrecurring Closing Costs Can Be Negotiable

There are two types of fees when buying a home:

    Recurring

    Nonrecurring

Recurring closing costs are costs that will occur again, on the same loan. Recurring closing costs are things like a home insurance policy and property taxes. Your lender will want to see an insurance policy in force when you buy the new home, but this is also a cost that you'll encounter again when your policy comes up for renewal.

So are your property taxes and mortgage interest. You will pay mortgage interest again each month, and you'll also pay property taxes again either once or twice per year, depending upon where you live.

These are costs that can't be controlled by your lender. Your lender won't provide you with a hazard insurance policy on the home in case of fire or storm; instead, you'll get both the quote and the policy from an insurance agent.

Likewise, your lender has nothing to do with your property taxes. Your property taxes are based upon the value of your home and are set by your local appraisal authority or taxing office.

What your lender does have control over is your interest charges, which are determined by your interest rate, your amount borrowed, and your loan term. These three items are recurring; they will happen again. And again.

CONFIDENTIAL: Watch the Nonrecurring Fees for Junk Fees

Nonrecurring closing charges are fees associated, specifically, with the closing of your deal. They will include payments to everyone from the appraiser to the surveyor and anyone else in between that will claim a piece of the action when it comes to your wallet.

Nonrecurring charges are the ones you need to be concerned about. Recurring charges are not. Nonrecurring charges are those collected by:

The lender

The appraiser

The credit agency

The attorney

The closer or escrow company

The home inspector

The title agency

Did I leave anyone out? Oh, yeah, I forgot:

County government

Other government fees, depending on where you live

Flood companies

Tax service companies

Pest inspection

Home warranties

Surveyors

Everyone else I missed who might show up on your credit report

So how do you prepare for such closing costs? You need to do a little homework. This book will answer all your questions, but what will happen is that your potential lender will provide you with a list of potential home loan fees in the form of an estimate.

Your lender is required to provide you with an estimate of closing fees within three business days after receipt of your loan application if you submitted your loan application by mail, fax, or online, and immediately if you made the application face-to-face. Your lender provides you with this list of potential charges in good faith. This means that, based on the lender's experience, local customs, and its estimate, your fees will total $XXXX.

In good faith. Estimate. That's why this is called the Good Faith Estimate of Settlement Charges.

This piece of paper is perhaps the one document that causes the most problems during the loan approval process. The Good Faith Estimate, or

GFE, is the loan officer's best guess as to what charges the buyer will ultimately be asked to pay for at the time of loan closing.

In addition to recurring and nonrecurring closing fees, the borrower will also be required to bring the down payment (if any) and perhaps verification of any additional cash reserves that a lender might require before issuing a final loan approval.

CONFIDENTIAL: Your Loan Officer Is Supposed to Advise You of Potential Charges, but the Estimate Doesn't Have to Be Accurate

That's because there is no universal guideline for what makes a "good" GFE and what makes a worthless one. There are certain guidelines for what sort of variance is acceptable and what is not, and most of those guidelines suggest that the final set of closing costs determined at closing must not exceed the original closing cost estimate by 1/8 percent of the amount borrowed. But there is no federal statute making that a requirement.

If the loan officer is off, so what? You can't sue him to get your money back unless the error was willful and made with an intent to deceive. If the loan officer says, "This loan will cost you $100," but when you go to closing, there is actually $10,000 in closing fees, that's an intent to deceive. Being off by a couple of thousand dollars might be just a bad estimate. Instead of bringing $8,000 to the closing table, you might have to bring $10,000, for instance.

Federal Truth in Lending Laws, which require lenders to calculate, among other things, the annual percentage rate, or APR, were designed to help consumers compare one lender to another and to help explain the various closing costs associated with a particular loan. In fact, these laws do require that anytime a lender advertises an interest rate for a mortgage loan, that same advertisement must disclose the APR right alongside the rate quote.

If you look closely at home loan ads, you'll see these APR numbers.

If you don't see them, the lender is in violation of federal lending laws, but most likely you'll see the APR. It's the APR that is used in the guideline: There is approximately 1/8 percent tolerance in the difference between the initial APR and the final APR disclosed at your loan settlement.

For instance, suppose you buy a $150,000 home and secure a 5.50 percent 30-year fixed-rate loan. After all appropriate finance charges are added up in order to calculate the APR, your rate figure might come in at a 5.72 percent APR. When you go to closing, you'll see your final APR figure on your Truth in Lending document. If your APR comes in at or below 1/8 percent above 5.72 percent, or 5.845 percent, then your final APR number is "within tolerance." But if it's higher than that, you're said to be "out of tolerance."

But again, this isn't something that's currently against any law. It's just bad business. You have to decide whether or not to take the loan with the higher fees, as expressed by the new APR number and your final settlement sheet of listed closing fees. If you choose not to take the loan, you walk away. Unfortunately, if you walk away, you could also lose your house and your earnest money deposit.

That's not a good situation to be in.

CONFIDENTIAL: Your Loan Officer Probably Can't Explain the APR Number

This might be a little "old school" on my part, because now such numbers are spewed out by a computer program. APR numbers are calculated by a software application and can vary depending on the day on which your loan closes. Really.

Correctly defined, the APR is the cost of money borrowed, expressed as an annual rate. That means that your mortgage loan wasn't free. First, your lender charged you interest. Your lender most likely will have also charged you other fees in addition to that interest, such as lender fees, appraisal charges, and maybe discount points or origination fees. The alleged benefit from comparing APRs from one lender to another is being able to discover additional lender charges that are being levied by either lender. For instance, Blue Bank offers 6.00 percent and no points. Red Bank offers 6.25 percent and no points. Easy, right? Run to Blue Bank. Not so fast. If the APR were examined, you might find that Blue Bank didn't charge any points, but it charged a 2 percent origination fee, $500 in junk lender fees, and an application fee to the tune of $400. Red Bank, on the other hand, required none of those additional fees. So while the note rate offered by Blue Bank was lower, the additional lender fees made the deal at Red Bank much better.

CONFIDENTIAL: Knowing What's Included in the APR Is Critical When Comparing Loans

APR numbers are best used to compare identical loans from one lender to another. The higher the APR number compared to the note rate, the more lender fees you're being charged. If you compare two competing APRs on identical loan programs, then the lower APR might be your best choice.

But knowing what is and what is not included in the APR number is critical in knowing whether or not you're getting screwed by the lender.

If you have a pencil handy, the correct way to calculate the APR of a mortgage loan is as follows. I'm not kidding.

First, you'll need to calculate the monthly payment.

$$M = P * \{J/[1 - (1 + J)^N]\}$$

where

M = mortgage payment
P = principal
J = monthly interest expressed as a decimal [$I/(12 \times 100)$]
N = number of months financed
I = interest rate

After you get that number, (it's okay to resharpen your pencil), subtract your finance charges from your principal (*P*) and recalculate for the interest payment (*J*). It's fairly easy to do if you've done it a few times.

Okay, I'll admit it: I've never done it that way, and it's likely that few people have. I always use a calculator. But I can do it. And your loan officer should also be able to do it, but I'll bet you a doughnut that your loan officer can't calculate your APR number by herself. She needs a computer program to do it for her.

The important part of this exercise is understanding that the APR number is important when comparing closing costs from one lender to another. Those loan officers or other pundits who claim that the APR number is worthless are simply not applying its utility properly.

CONFIDENTIAL: The APR Can Be Useful Only When Comparing Identical Loan Programs

This is the main reason that many loan officers dismiss the value of the APR number: They mistakenly assume that you can use the APR to compare absolutely all mortgage loan programs at once and pick out the best one simply by looking at the lower APR.

That's a mistake. If you get this explanation of how the APR is used from your loan officer, that loan officer had better be very, very good in other areas, because he's flat out wrong in this one. Here is the kind of thing you're likely to hear: "The APR is useless because for loans with less than 20 percent down, it assumes that mortgage insurance will be on the loan for the entire loan term."

That's true. That is the assumption in the calculation. But that doesn't necessarily mean that the APR is wrong; it only means that it uses a mortgage insurance premium in the calculation. Remember, anything that is required from the lender to get a mortgage must be included in the APR number.

The trick is to use the APR when looking at identical loans. If one loan needs mortgage insurance, then the next one from another lender will too, so the APRs should be a useful tool.

"The APR doesn't work when comparing adjustable mortgages to fixed rates."

Again, that's true. We'll explore the wide, wide world of available mortgage loans in Chapter 7, but that's not how you compare them. Adjustable-rate mortgages use what is termed the *fully indexed rate* when calculating the APR number. It's a different number. You may get an adjustable-rate mortgage that starts out at 4.00 percent, but that may not be the number used to calculate the APR.

But again that's off the mark. The APR works only when comparing like loans. And a fixed rate and an ARM are not alike. The APR doesn't work right when you try to compare loans this way.

In the real world, you'll speak to loan officers with various levels of experience. Meaning, of course, that you could get some very wild data. What do you do?

If you're getting APR quotes that vary significantly from one another, or if you're simply tired of all the disclosure stuff, try another method: Get closing cost quotes from your prospective lenders, and pay no attention to any closing fee that's not from your lenders.

In addition to the difference between recurring and nonrecurring fees, there is also a difference between nonrecurring fees that involve lender charges and nonlender charges. Lenders can control what they charge, but they cannot control what an independent third party charges.

CONFIDENTIAL: Loan Officers Can Low-Ball Third-Party Fees to Make Their Loan Offering Look Better

This might be one of the biggest con games in the business. But let's think about the dynamics of all this, so that it will make sense.

When you get ready to compare lenders and you get your GFE, what is the normal tendency? Do you first look at each individual item? No,

you jump to the bottom line where it says "total closing costs." Loan officers know this. And they play this game every day. You don't. I'll give you
an example.

You contact two lenders. Each lender quotes a similar interest rate
and similar lender fees, but third-party fees vary considerably. Third-party
fees include such nonlender fees as attorneys, title insurance, surveys,
escrow, and settlement charges.

Each loan officer faxes over to you his GFE, and you first review all
fees associated with the lender (these fees are listed first, at the very top
of the GFE). Lender A quotes:

Discount point	$2,000
Appraisal	$ 350
Credit report	$ 22
Tax service	$ 72
Flood certificate	$ 15
Processing	$ 300
Underwriting	$ 550
Total	$ 3,209

These are common lender fees. Lender B quotes:

Discount point	$2,000
Appraisal	$ 350
Credit report	$ 15
Tax service	$ 72
Flood certificate	$ 15
Processing	$ 200
Underwriting	$ 200
Administrative	$ 200
Total	$ 3,052

So far, so good, right? These two competing lenders are quoting similar closing costs, and really the difference between them isn't all that
great. Lender A appears to be about $200 or so more expensive than
Lender B.

But the GFE doesn't just include charges from the lender. It also includes any and all charges that you might anticipate from third parties, including attorney charges, taxes, title insurance, surveys, settlement fees, and anything else that is usual or customary in your area.

In this case, though, the GFEs take a remarkable turn from one another. Lender A goes on to quote:

Attorney	$ 100
Title insurance	$ 500
Escrow	$ 150
Document prep	$ 150
Survey	$ 250
Total nonlender fees	$ 1,150

Lender B also continues with its quote:

Attorney	$ 200
Title insurance	$ 500
Escrow	$ 250
Document prep	$ 250
Survey	$ 400
Total nonlender fees	$ 1,650

At this point, Lender A looks better when quoting nonlender fees by $500. Now, when you add everything together:

Lender A	$ 4,359
Lender B	$ 4,702

Looks like Lender A is the way to go, right? Guess what, you were low-balled on the nonlender charges. Nonlender charges are what they are and have no bearing on what your loan officer quotes you.

But if you are an unwary consumer, you will go to your closing, review your final settlement statement, and see the actual charges issued by the attorney, the title company, and everyone else. The charges are nowhere near what Lender A quoted you—in fact they're off by about $500.

So you protest: "Hey, these aren't the fees quoted by my loan officer. You're charging too much!"

"No, I'm sorry," says the attorney. "I've always charged $200, and all of the rest of these fees are in line as well."

What has just happened is that you were taken. Not only did Lender A misquote these fees to you on purpose, but now you must pay the actual charges warranted by your closing. And you must also pay Lender A its higher closing costs. Lender B was the better deal, because it was honest about nonlender fees, but once you get to closing, it's too late.

How do you protect yourself from all of this? It's difficult, I know. Who in the world would know how much an escrow fee costs other than an escrow company? Or how about title insurance—how much is that? The fact is that none of these fees are common knowledge among consumers. A gallon of milk? Sure. A gallon of gas? You bet. But a survey? Come on!

You protect yourself by reviewing the GFEs you've received. If one lender is much lower than anyone else and those low quotes are for third-party services, then you can do two things:

1. Pick up the phone and call your Realtor.
2. Call the various services being quoted directly and ask them how much they charge.

CONFIDENTIAL: Realtors Have a Stake in Making Sure That You Are Not Screwed

When you are working with a Realtor, you can call a halt to a lot of these shenanigans. If you're working with a local loan officer and not an online lender, then your loan officer depends upon her reputation in the Realtor community. If your loan officer messes up too many times, you can bet that Realtors will steer their clients away from her.

If you use a Realtor referral, your Realtor has put his reputation at risk. Realtors don't like to do that. If you get a referral from a Realtor and something bad happens, you don't just blame the bad person you were referred to; you also blame the Realtor for giving you a bad referral. Realtors live and die by the referral.

When you get a GFE from a loan officer, let your Realtor take a look at it. Let your Realtor see if certain charges are being quoted correctly. In most instances, you have no control over where your closing will take place or who the seller's title insurance company will be or how much the document preparation people will charge for their services. Often it's the Realtor who decides who gets a lot of this business.

So if you're scheduled to have your closing at XYZ Escrow Company and two lenders are quoting two different fees for the very same service at the very same company, then someone's wrong. Right? In fact, it's possible that they'll both be wrong. When you ask your Realtor to review what you've been quoted, you're relying on the Realtor's personal experience with the escrow firm, not on a GFE issued by someone who's never used the escrow firm in question.

CONFIDENTIAL: You Can Call Companies Directly to See if Their Fees Are Accurately Quoted on an Estimate

You're not using a Realtor or your Realtor isn't familiar with certain settlement fees? Then pick up the phone and ask the company directly. If you're in certain areas of the country where you get to choose your own attorney, then the attorney fees will be accurately quoted. In other parts of the United States, an attorney is involved, but she doesn't act on your behalf; instead, she represents the lender, reviews papers, or holds a settlement.

If you're not sure what an attorney charges in these cases, pick up the phone and ask. "Hi, this is David Reed, and I'm scheduled to close with your firm. What do you charge?"

You'll get an answer, which you can then compare with what has been provided you by your various lenders. If you see one lender who sticks out as being the most consistent in its rate quotes, you should seriously consider doing business with that lender. If a lender is telling you the truth about various fees from third parties while everyone else seems to be all over the map, I would trust that lender with everything else.

CONFIDENTIAL: "Guaranteed" Closing Costs Don't Mean That the Whole Estimate Is Guaranteed

Okay, with the dawn of disclosure in the form of the GFE comes the expected, "Okay, we know we should have been giving you accurate closing cost quotes all along, but this time we guarantee that we'll get it right!"

What a concept, right? Can you imagine this type of cost chicanery in another industry? I can't think of one.

"Hi, can you tell me the cost of that bicycle?"

"Sure; it's between $500 and $800."

"Well, which is it, $500 or $800?"

"We can't tell you exactly until you get to the cash register to pay."

Can you believe it? You want to know the price of something, but you don't get it until it's time to open your checkbook?

"Pardon me, I'd like to know what you would charge to represent me in my legal case."

"Sure; I charge anywhere from $100 an hour to $700 per hour."

"But I want to know how much you're going to charge before I decide to use you."

"Sorry, but I can only give you an estimate."

That's the problem with the good faith estimate; it's only an estimate. If it's mildly off, you grin and bear it, and if it's wildly off, you don't grin and possibly lose the deal entirely.

But along comes closing cost "guarantees." A lender will guarantee its closing costs. Only in lending, right?

But there are two types of such guarantees floating around in the marketplace:

Lender guarantees

One-fee guarantees

Lender guarantees are the more common variety of lender closing cost guarantees. They essentially mean that the lender will quote you some closing costs and guarantee that they'll be accurate.

But what is this lender guaranteeing, and, more importantly, what is the guarantee? Do you get a free loan or something?

There are lenders who have gotten themselves in trouble by advertising "guaranteed closing costs," but the fine print points out that they don't guarantee anything but their own closing costs and the guarantee applies to no one else's charges. That means that the lender can mostly do whatever it wants with regard to quoting nonlender charges as long as it gets its own fees right.

Big deal. Lenders certainly should know their own closing costs. It's like asking their name. What's your name? "Big Lender." What are your closing costs? "$799."

There should be no fudge factor when lenders quote their own fees. Heck, the fees are all over their rate sheets for their loan officers to quote their customers. But okay, what if the lender's fees are quoted incorrectly? What exactly happens? Does the lender give you a million dollars?

Of course not. The lender simply makes the adjustment at closing, and you're on your way to closing. A lender guarantee on closing costs is nothing more than a marketing gimmick. It's like the lender guaranteeing its mailing address. It's not a bad idea by any stretch; it's the notion of guaranteeing something that should be taken as a given that's ridiculous.

CONFIDENTIAL: "One-Fee" Costs Aren't Necessarily Higher or Lower Than Itemized Costs

On the other hand, there are lenders that guarantee more than just their fees, but they do it in a special way, and that way is called "one fee." One-fee lenders quote you one big, fat, happy number and stick to it. And this number includes all fees, not just the lenders' fees.

This is a new concept that makes a lot of sense but has yet to catch on in a major way, mainly because it gives mortgage bankers the upper hand. A mortgage banker can contact various affiliate suppliers, such as appraisers or title insurers, and strike a deal with them, such as, "If we give you this business, will you discount it?" The lender can then add up all the quoted fees and charge the total to the borrower.

Instead of itemizing 30 different charges on a settlement statement, all adding up to a particular number, the lender says, "$3,800." Now the borrower doesn't have to spend hours comparing one lender's fees with another's or calling attorneys or escrow companies asking for a particular rate quote, but instead gets one number: $3,800. That number doesn't guarantee a lower total closing cost outlay; it just lets you know exactly what you're going to pay.

CONFIDENTIAL: Sometimes Major Closing Cost Errors Are Made by Incompetent Loan Officers

This may sound like a given, but there's a difference between being a crook and being stupid. A crook will lie to your face, whereas someone who's stupid simply may not know any better.

There are common closing cost misquotes, and often those misquotes involve not reporting mortgage interest, taxes or insurance properly—all recurring closing fees.

Property taxes aren't readily known by your loan officer but have to be guessed at when the loan officer compiles the GFE. Good loan officers will know the approximate property tax rates and quote accordingly. Good loan officers will also know estimated home insurance quotes. But they also have to quote an item called "prepaid interest."

Prepaid interest is interest paid ahead of time, to the lender. There is only one time that the lender accepts prepaid interest, and that is with a brand new mortgage loan. To understand prepaid interest, one must first understand the difference between rent payments and mortgage payments.

Rent is paid in advance. When you pay rent on the first of the month, you're paying for the month you're about to live in the property. When you pay mortgage interest, it's always paid in "arrears," or backwards. When you make a mortgage payment on the first of every month, you're paying for the previous month's accumulated daily interest charges.

Your lender will add up your per diem interest from the day of your closing to the first of the following month.

Let's say you have a 7.00 percent 30-year rate on a $200,000 loan. That gives you a $1,330 monthly payment, which divided by 30 days equals $44.35. Thus, $44.35 is the daily interest accrual. Your closing is taking place on the 25th of the month, so your new lender will collect daily interest up to the first of the next month, or six days. Six days times $44.35 equals $266.10. This is the amount of the prepaid interest on your new mortgage.

The next time you make a mortgage payment, it will be on the first of yet the next month, and this time it will cover a full month's worth of interest.

When a loan officer calculates your GFE, there is a space where daily interest accrued is listed. Many loan officers keep this figure as low as possible, again to make their closing cost estimate look better. If your loan officer calculates that your closing will take place on the very last day of the month, your prepaid interest will be for only one day—in this example, $44.35.

If the contract on your new home states a closing date of the tenth of the month and you don't get a new GFE, then you'll be surprised at the new, higher amount of $887, not the $44.35 originally disclosed. Rookie loan officers can sometimes overlook this issue and not warn you of how the money due at closing can change based upon when you actually close your loan.

CONFIDENTIAL: Estimates for Property Taxes and Insurance Are Often Wrong

Another common mistake is similar to interest errors, and that is miscalculating property taxes. Exact property taxes are typically available only through public records or through tax data published in a local multiple listing service. But most experienced loan officers know the average tax rates for the area and can give you a solid quote.

The same goes with hazard insurance. A standard estimate of hazard insurance is about $^{1}/_{2}$ percent of the mortgage balance, but of course the exact number will come not from the loan officer, but from the buyer's chosen insurance company. Fair enough, mistakes can be made when estimating, but when it comes time to calculate the amount to be placed in escrow or impound accounts, that amount will be compounded by the mistake.

Escrow accounts, sometimes called impound accounts, are deposit accounts established by the home buyer to pay annual property tax bills and insurance premiums. Depending upon the lending institution, a lender may ask for a couple of months' worth of insurance and taxes to get the impound account started.

When an impound or escrow account is set up, each month the borrower adds 1/12 of the annual tax and insurance payments to the mortgage payment; as those bills become due the following year, the lender takes those deposited funds and pays the tax bill and insurance premium on behalf of the homeowners. It's quite a good deal, actually: You never have to worry about whether the insurance is paid up or whether there is enough money to pay the property taxes when they come due. Whether or not to establish escrow and impound accounts is usually at the discretion of the borrower, but they are almost always required when the buyer's first mortgage loan represents more than 80 percent of the sales price of the property.

So if the insurance policy is low-balled and the property taxes are misquoted, it can be quite a shock when you get to the closing table and have to come up with not just higher taxes and insurance than you were quoted, but at least double the amount of the error.

CONFIDENTIAL: Mortgage Brokers Have a More Difficult Time Quoting Accurate Closing Fees Than Mortgage Bankers

The reason for this is that your mortgage broker may not yet know where your loan will end up. Just as mortgage lenders can have different lender fees, so can wholesale lenders. In fact, wholesale lenders have different sets of fees for the very same reason that mortgage brokers or bankers have different fee charges: to make them appear different.

All in all, the fees may not be called the same thing, but you can bet that they'll be there. Common lender fees, wholesale or otherwise, can include:

Processing. This charge covers the physical work it takes to push your loan through the approval channels. Common charge: $300.

Underwriting. This is a fee charged to offset the costs associated with making sure that the loan application conforms to the lender's approval guidelines. Common charge: $300–$400.

Administrative. It's not clear what this fee does, but it's not an uncommon one. It's an official-sounding term that's really nothing more than a junk charge. Common charge: $200–$300.

Application. This fee, when charged, is usually collected up front, at application time. Often this fee goes toward paying the appraisal or credit report charges, but it doesn't have to. Common charge: $300.

Rarely will you encounter every single one of these fees from the same lender; instead, you will see a combination of them, and perhaps even some more creative ones. But the important thing is not what a fee is or is not called, but what all the fees actually add up to. Some lenders charge an administrative fee and some don't.

That's why a mortgage broker may not be able to be as close in quoting lender fees unless your broker knows ahead of time specifically who that loan will go to. If your broker knows who your lender will be, you'll get an accurate quote. If the broker doesn't know or hasn't decided, it's possible that the estimate will be off by a few hundred dollars—at least, until your final lender is identified.

CONFIDENTIAL: There Is No Such Thing as a "No-Closing-Cost" Mortgage Loan

You've seen the ads, and you probably wonder how some lenders can offer a no-closing-cost loan when others can't. The fact is that there isn't any such animal. And there are two ways that consumers can be misled if they're not careful.

One way is that when the lender offers a no-closing-cost loan, it is talking only about its own charges and not anyone else's. A lender may offer a loan program that has no fees, but the fees the lender is talking about may be processing or underwriting or other junk lender charges.

When you see a lender ad claiming "no closing costs," there might be an asterisk somewhere stating, "No lender fees; other fees will apply." Or the advertisement might say "No lender fees!" While this is certainly closer to the truth, you also need to be aware that lenders can offset waiving certain junk fees by increasing the interest rate.

But a real no-cost loan means that you pay no money for anything: no appraisal fees, title insurance, attorney—whatever it is, you don't pay for it. At least, not outright. Here is a list of common nonlender charges:

Title insurance	$ 500
Attorney	$ 300
Survey	$ 400
Documents	$ 200
Settlement	$ 500
Total	$ 1,900

Somebody is going to have to pay these folks. They have to pay their bills, too, don't they? Well if you're not going to pay them with a no-closing-cost loan, then who pays them? The lender will have to. But the lender can't really afford to do that, at least not for very long if it keeps giving loans away and paying all its clients' closing costs.

Instead, the lender will offer to pay these charges in exchange for a higher interest rate. Here's how it works.

First, add up your closing costs; in this case, let's say $1,900. Now divide that figure by the loan amount you're getting from your lender. Let's say you're borrowing $250,000. So $1,900 divided by $250,000 = 0.008, or 0.8 percent. That represents nearly 1 discount point, and while 1 discount point will drop your interest rate by $1/4$ percent, raising your interest rate by $1/4$ percent means that you get nearly 1 "point" coming back to you, in this case, 0.08 percent of $250,000, or $1,900.

You agree to pay a higher interest rate in exchange for not paying any closing costs. Is this a no-closing-cost loan? Of course not. It's a higher cost that you pay each month in the form of a higher payment.

There is no free lunch when it comes to closing costs. You pay them in one way or another.

CONFIDENTIAL: Sometimes Lenders Will Let You Borrow Your Closing Costs

When you are refinancing, this is no big deal. In fact, most refinancings roll the closing costs into the loan. We'll look at refinancing in greater detail in Chapter 8. There are a couple of ways to let you do it in a purchase transaction, but the main one is by taking a special loan program that allows such a practice.

Not only do these loans allow buyers to roll their closing costs in with their purchase transaction, but they are also zero-down loans. Not a bad day's work, is it? A home loan with no money down and no closing costs as well?

There are a few programs, albeit a very few, that allow you to do just that. They're typically called "103s."

Each loan represents the total loan-to-value of the property being purchased. If a home sells for $100,000 and the buyer puts zero down but still has closing costs of, say $3,000, the lender will allow a loan that goes up to 103 percent of the value of the home, hence the 103 moniker.

There are a very few loan programs that allow buyers to roll up to 7 percent of the sales price of the home into the loan amount for purposes of buying the house. In fact, there is just one variation of the 107 that I know of, but it is offered by different lenders. It's not a very attractive loan in terms of rate and program, but it's out there.

The more prolific of the two, yet still uncommon, is the 103 program. It is a conventional loan in that it is a Freddie Mac product. This program allows a second mortgage loan to rest behind the first, and this loan can include closing costs. This product may require that you live in certain areas or that your income not exceed certain income limits. Such programs are designed to foster home ownership for those without a down payment and closing costs, but they're out there.

C H A P T E R   5

Interest Rates

Mortgage interest rates can be a mystery. Why are one lender's rates so much lower than another's? Or, conversely, why are one lender's rates so much higher? Consumers can get an immediate price quote on nearly every consumer item on the market, from the cost of gasoline to the price of an airplane ticket. Mortgages aren't like that.

Mortgage rates are set each and every morning by the various mortgage companies. That's right, every morning. And they can change throughout the day. If you understand how mortgage rates are set and what affects them, you'll be prepared if a lender seems to quote one thing and offer another.

CONFIDENTIAL: The Mortgage Rates You See in the Newspaper Are Never Reliable

This means that you can never lock in the rate you see in the newspaper. Most Sunday newspapers carry a weekly mortgage rate survey from various lenders; it can be in the form of an advertisement, or the newspaper can actually pick up the telephone and call various lenders to get a rate quote.

Either way, the quotes are inaccurate at best.

These so-called rate surveys must be completed by the newspaper typically no later than the Thursday before the Sunday paper runs. Thus, the rates you see are at least that old. In fact, if you call up a lender advertising cheap rates, you'll find out that those rates aren't there—they were good only on the date the information was gathered.

The very same thing can be said about mortgage rate advertisements in general. You see them everywhere. You can see them the sports section of a newspaper, you can hear them on the radio, and you can even see them on billboards or nailed to utility poles.

So what good are these rate surveys? Not much, really, but you need to understand the dynamics at play here. Mortgage companies that list their interest rates alongside other lenders' rates know one thing: that people who look at such information are doing so to compare one lender with the next. What's the point of advertising your interest rates if you're the highest? You could get a reputation for being the highest lender in town.

The point of advertising rates is to get new business from consumers who are looking for low rates. Do consumers shop for the highest rates? Of course not. Knowing those things, mortgage companies must quote low, low rates.

The companies also know, of course, that should the consumer actually contact the lending company and want to lock in those rates, the response from the loan officer will be something like:

"Oh, I'm sorry, those rates were available last week, but I'm afraid the market has moved since then. But since you've called, tell me . . ." And so on. The lender's advertisement is doing what any good advertising is supposed to do—generate leads. The salesperson (your loan officer) takes it from there.

Is this "bait and switch"? Probably. If in fact you can get the interest rate that is advertised, then it's not. But if the rate being quoted in an advertisement isn't available for some reason, then either rates have moved since then or that rate was never really there.

CONFIDENTIAL: Mortgage Rates Advertised on the Internet Are Also Inaccurate

The problem with print ads is that they can be several days old. However, even the up-to-date advertisements one can find on the Internet, those that can be updated within a few minutes, also fall victim to the same issue.

Here is the challenge with rates found on the Internet. The rates look good. Often, they look very, very good. So go ahead and do some homework to show you that I'm right. This weekend, pick up a newspaper and look at some mortgage rate quotes from lenders in your area. They'll be relatively low.

Now log onto a web site and search for mortgage quotes. Those rates will be even lower than the ones you saw in the newspaper. Why is that, you wonder?

Just as companies that advertise in the newspaper must compete against their own local competitors using nothing more than interest rates, those that compete on the Internet must compete with the whole universe of mortgage lenders that also advertise on the Internet. Lenders who advertise in rate surveys must quote the lowest rate they possibly can—perhaps even rates lower than they can realistically offer. Why?

Because by the time you contact them, the rates may no longer be available. Are you skeptical?

I know how these things work. I've advertised on the Internet and in local newspapers. I've seen low-ball quotes from other lenders that were simply unbelievable. I know how interest rates are set, and I read all the columns in newspaper articles and on the Web that are flat-out wrong.

Why all this confusion? Because mortgage rates can change by the second, and your lender knows it.

CONFIDENTIAL: The Federal Reserve Has Nothing to Do with Your Mortgage Rate

Mortgage rates aren't set by the government. They're not issued by the Fed. And perhaps the most often-quoted myth is that rates are tied to the 30-year Treasury bond or the 10-year Treasury note. Sorry, everyone, they're not. In fact, mortgage rates aren't set by any one person or organization; they're set by you and me. They're set by open markets that bid on the price of various bonds—mortgage bonds.

Mortgage rates are tied to their specific index; 30-year rates are tied to a 30-year mortgage bond, and 15-year rates are tied to a 15-year mortgage bond. Conventional loans and government loans both have their indexes. And it's the selling and buying of these bond traders, public and private investors, that set market rates. Let's explain this a little further by first seeing how bonds work in general. If you understand how bonds work, you'll understand both how and when rates are set. In fact, you'll probably know more about this process than your loan officer does.

Bonds are an investment vehicle, and unlike stocks, another investment vehicle, they are predictable. There is no guessing about what the price of a bond will be at its maturity. Perhaps the most familiar bond is the U.S. Savings Bond. And this is a good way to begin to understand how mortgage bonds operate.

If you were to go out and buy a $100 U.S. Savings Bond today, it would cost you $50 for a common series U.S. bond. No, you wouldn't able to buy a $100 bond for $50, then turn around the next day and sell it for $100. Instead, you would have to wait a certain period of time, predetermined by the bond maturity itself, before you could get that $100.

How long do you have to wait? It depends upon the bond. For a 30-year bond, you would wait until 30 years have passed to get your $100.

That works out to just over a 3.00 percent return on investment. Not a whopping return like the one on your Google stock? No, not at all. But bonds aren't that type of investment; instead, they're considered more secure. You are guaranteed a rate of return at a specified time.

That's on a global, or "macro," level. On an individual, or "micro," level, here's what mortgage bond traders do all day long, every business day: They buy and sell mortgage bonds.

Since bonds are predictable, the return isn't that sexy. Instead, bond owners invest because of the guarantee; they don't want any surprises. But who would invest in a mortgage bond when there are other investment opportunities that could pay much more? Those who either don't like risk or want to offset the risk of other investments.

When the stock market is going crazy and it seems as if everyone is investing something in stocks to get a great return, investors typically pull their money out of those staid bonds and use that cash to buy high-flying stocks. Remember the dot-com boom? Real estate?

Bonds must compete for those same investment dollars, and when money is pulled out of a mortgage bond to chase higher earnings elsewhere, the seller of those bonds must make adjustments in the price of the bond. The lower demand means that the price will be lower. And a lower price means a higher return, or yield, on that bond.

When there are fewer buyers of a fixed note, the sellers have to lower the price of that note to attract buyers, which also increases the yield on that note.

What causes a price to go up or down? The demand. If the stock market is tanking, then investors might want to sell stocks and put more money into the safe return guaranteed by bonds. But if more people want the same thing, then guess what happens? That's right, the price goes up because of the increased demand. A bondholder can get more money for the same bond. When the price goes up, the yield, or return, goes down.

On the other hand, if people pull money out of bonds and move it into stocks, it's because the economy is moving along at a good pace and investors expect a better return. When the price of a bond falls, the yield goes up.

The Fed has nothing to do with your mortgage rate.

CONFIDENTIAL: The Fed Attempts to Control Inflation and the Cost of Money, Not Your Mortgage

There's always a lot of talk and speculation about "what the Fed will do" at its next meeting, and newspapers and reporters hang on every word a Fed governor says at some luncheon that might give some hint of future Fed actions.

The Fed does have an impact on the economy, certainly. But its impact is related to the cost of money—specifically, to two key indexes: the federal funds rate and the federal discount rate.

The federal funds rate, or fed funds, is the rate at which banks lend to one another. Why do banks do that? Banks have *reserve requirements*, meaning that at the end of the day, a bank needs to have cash reserves that are a certain percentage of its amount of loans outstanding.

Just as any rate can be affected by market forces, such as banks competing to lend money to other banks that want it, the fed funds rate is actually a "target" or goal set by the Fed, but it is generally adhered to by banks that lend to and borrow from one another.

So how does raising or lowering the fed funds rate affect the economy in general? If money is cheap, lenders will be more inclined to make loans, stimulating a possibly weak economy. In times when the economy is overheating, leading to inflation, increased rates can reduce the demand for money, making it more expensive. When money is more expensive, businesses and consumers alike are less likely to borrow.

This money control attempts to keep inflation in check.

The discount rate is similar in nature to the fed funds rate, except that this rate is the rate set by the Federal Reserve for lending to commercial banks, again on a short-term basis and again to make reserve adjustments.

Both indexes can affect the economy, which can affect mortgage rates, but there is no direct correlation.

CONFIDENTIAL: The Prime Rate at One Bank Can Be Different from the Prime Rate at Another

One caveat here: Mortgage loans based upon a bank's prime rate will be directly affected by the bank's own cost of funds. The prime rate is what banks charge their very, very best customers. While the Fed doesn't adjust a bank's prime rate, it adjusts the rate at which banks can lend money. The prime rate will always be higher than the discount rate and the fed funds rate.

The prime rate is defined by the *Wall Street Journal* (*WSJ*) as "The base rate on corporate loans posted by at least 75% of the nation's 30 largest banks." One bank's prime rate might be different from another bank's.

Loans that are based on a bank's prime rate are typically adjustable (like the index) mortgages. Equity loans and second mortgages are almost always of this type. We'll discuss equity lending in more detail in Chapter 8.

CONFIDENTIAL: A Lender's "Secondary Department" Sets Mortgage Rates for Its Company

Every single day, all day long, there is a department at a mortgage company that does nothing except watch the prices of various mortgage bonds to determine how the company will set its mortgage rates for the day. This department is called the *secondary department* of the lender, and every mortgage banking operation has one. It's this department that sets the rates that are distributed to the company's loan officers, who pass them along to you, the consumer.

As each business day opens, all of these secondary departments watch the opening trading of the various mortgage bonds. If the price of the 30-year Fannie Mae bond is selling on the open market at the same price as yesterday, then the rates for that day will be the same.

If the price of the bond goes up, the yield then goes down, meaning that rates get lower. If there is less demand for a mortgage bond, the yield goes up, raising mortgage rates. This goes on all day long. And mortgage prices change constantly.

Mortgage bonds are priced in basis points; 1 basis point equals $1/100$ of 1 percent. As the price of a bond changes throughout the day, the secondary department must be alert for any price swings. If the price of a particular mortgage bond moves by just a few points, say three or four, there will be no change.

If, however, there is a move in price of, say, 15 or more basis points, you can expect the lender to make a price adjustment. Different lenders may have different thresholds for price changes, but most will start to get nervous if bond prices have moved 15 basis points one way or another. You can bet that if the bond price has changed by 15 or more basis points, there will be a midday rate change. This is why rates seen in the newspaper, on the Internet, or in other advertisements mean little—they change.

The rates themselves generally won't change as much as the cost to the consumer will change. If 6.00 percent can be found at 1 discount point and mortgage bonds lose 50 basis points, that will typically mean an adjustment in interest rate to 6.125 percent or cost you, the consumer, $1/2$ discount point more in price. Don't confuse basis points with discount points. They're different.

Secondary departments watch mortgage bond pricing, and also watch for various economic and political events that might trigger a bond selloff or a bond rally. Did the unemployment number show strong job gains? Then one can expect money to move out of bonds and into stocks. That means higher rates.

Economic events that point to a stronger or weaker economy will also affect interest rates throughout the day. So can political events.

Events at home or abroad can affect mortgage rates. Anything that could be interpreted as being a drag on the economy would portend lower rates. Is there uncertainty in any particular market? Then look for an economy that is not poised to move in one direction or another. And in most cases, whenever there is uncertainty, stock markets move lower and more money is put into bonds.

Then again, economic or political news can have no impact on markets. Or conflicting news items can "cancel" each item out, keeping rates stable. Typically, rates won't have extended periods of wild swings. There will be some adjustments as market moods shift, but overall one won't be seeing constant, dramatic rate changes. But change they can, and that's why the rates you see advertised anywhere aren't reliable.

CONFIDENTIAL: It's Imperative to Get Rate Quotes on the Same Day at the Same Time

When you begin getting mortgage quotes, you must remember how and when rates can change. They can change at any time. Do you spend all day long looking at mortgage bond pricing, analyzing economic reports, and listening to CNN in the background? No, you don't. But lenders do.

Secondary departments don't like surprises, and they are ready at the helm to adjust an interest rate should markets begin to move. Knowing this dynamic, you have to begin and end your rate search in as short a time as possible.

Mortgage rates are usually issued around 11:00 a.m. EST. Some lenders will price earlier, some later, but they all price after the markets have been open for a while. Lenders all watch the same data, listen to the same news, and follow the same reports. And price from the very same mortgage bond.

It is for this reason that you can't find one lender who is at 6.00 percent while everyone else is at 7.00 percent. Lenders price from the same index, and the difference between 6.00 percent and 7.00 percent is usually about 400 basis points. On a $500,000 mortgage, that equals $20,000. Lenders aren't that far apart. At best, the difference may be ¹/₄ percent. At best.

If you're seeing that most lenders are quoting one rate, give or take a bit, and another lender is way, way out of the ballpark, then there's something seriously wrong.

Because rates are issued at the same time each business morning, lenders usually come out with their rates at about the same time each day. That's when you need to make your calls when you're getting mortgage quotes. Don't bother calling before 10:00 a.m. EST; most lenders won't have their pricing for that day ready, and they won't let you lock in the previous day's rates.

But once you begin calling various lenders for rate quotes, don't waste a lot of time. Call everyone at as close to the same time as possible. If you spread your rate quote information out over the full day, or, worse yet, over several days, you could be making bad comparisons.

For instance, you wake up bright and early in the morning, determined to nail down a mortgage company that day. You get your pencil and paper, get your phone numbers, and begin calling. You contact several lenders and get some quotes, but one company hasn't returned your call.

Later that day, the company that has yet to quote for you calls and quotes you an interest rate. Perhaps you got 7.00 percent from three different lenders, but this lender is quoting something a little lower—6.75 percent.

Instead of celebrating, you need to make a note of that quote and immediately contact the other lenders to see if there have been any rate changes. If there had been a mortgage bond rally during the course of the day, then the lender quoting in the afternoon could be quoting from fresh rates, whereas the quotes you got in the morning didn't reflect that rate move. It's possible that everyone's rates went down during the day; you just didn't know about it.

If you get a rate quote that is $1/4$ percent or more better than anyone else's and you got that rate quote at a completely different time of the day or, worse, on a different day, call all the other lenders back and get another quote.

CONFIDENTIAL: Mortgage Bond Pricing Isn't Available to the General Public

Unlike quotes on other bonds, particularly bonds, notes, and bills issued by local, state, and federal governments, mortgage bond quotes aren't readily available to the public. There is no web site where one can go to get current mortgage bond pricing. There are several web sites that lenders can subscribe to that contain bond pricing, but secondary departments typically get their mortgage bond pricing directly from the bond traders or securities firms.

This information can get pricey; depending upon how often a lender wants to be updated on bond prices, it can cost $5,000 per year, or more, to have access to those data. There are companies that put people on the trading floor to follow bond buying and selling and relay that information to their customers.

Lenders don't want their consumers to have access to the same live data that they have. If they did, and there was a sudden turn toward the negative, consumers could call their loan officer and immediately lock in their interest rate before the lender has had time to make an interest-rate change. If a consumer gets quoted 7.00 percent and locks in the rate as rates begin moving to 7.25 percent, the consumer beats the lender by $1/4$ percent.

Sounds great, doesn't it? Unfortunately for you, that scenario will rarely happen—unless, of course, you're in the stock or bond business and have access to such information.

CONFIDENTIAL: Mortgage Rates Aren't Tied to the 10-Year Treasury Note or the 30-Year Treasury Bond

You will hear from various sources, incorrect ones, that mortgage rates are tied to the 10-year Treasury note or the 30-year Treasury bond. In fact, one can hear or read that information so often that it's taken for a fact. But it's not the case. Lenders don't base their rates on the 10-year Treasury note, or on any government bond. Period.

Okay, there will be some similar moves. Investors who like 10-year Treasuries or other longer-term bonds and those who invest in mortgage bonds are probably kindred spirits. The theory behind buying a 10-year Treasury is the same as that behind buying a mortgage bond. It's a flight to safety when there's economic trouble ahead.

But there is no direct correlation. Saying they move in parallel is stretching it. If your loan officer—or anyone else, for that matter, but especially your loan officer—tells you that rates follow the 10-year or 30-year Treasury, then you need to either politely tell her that that's not correct or find another loan officer you can trust. Why would a loan officer tell you something that's simply wrong and not know it? Wouldn't you want someone who knows that? Is there something else the loan officer might be wrong about?

Mortgage bonds are fixed instruments, so they're tied to fixed rates. What are adjustable-rate mortgages tied to, and how are they set? They're set in the very same way, by market forces. We'll discuss the various types of mortgage rates in Chapter 7, but adjustable rates work the same way that fixed rates work—lenders price them off of the exact same index.

CONFIDENTIAL: Adjustable-Rate Mortgage Indexes Are Easy to Follow; Fixed-Rate Ones Are Not

One difference however between a fixed-rate and an adjustable-rate mortgage is that the indexes used for adjustable-rate mortgages are widely available to the general public; they are probably listed in your newspaper right now if you look for them. Common adjustable-rate indexes are the one-year Treasury index, the six-month Treasury, six-month LIBOR, and six-month CD—practically any universally traded index could be used to set an adjustable rate.

CONFIDENTIAL: When Getting Rate Quotes, Get Quotes on the Exact Same Rate, Term, and Type

If a lender is not competitive on your loan program, she'll steer you in another direction.

While the APR is a useful tool for comparing rates and fees from different lenders, it's really effective only when comparing loans that are exactly alike. A 30-year mortgage from Blue Bank can be compared with a 30-year mortgage from Red Bank, but not with a 15-year mortgage from Yellow Bank.

An APR of 5.125 percent on a 15-year loan is incomprehensible when compared to an APR of 6.36 percent on a 30-year loan. And don't even think about comparing adjustable-rate mortgages with fixed rates.

If you've decided which loan program you want, use that loan program to get rate quotes and stick to it. Don't change. Changing the program is the oldest trick in the loan officer's book. If you call to get a rate quote for a 15-year fixed-rate loan, but the loan officer suggests other programs instead, then you'll know what's going on.

"Hi, I'd like to get your rate quote today for a 15-year fixed rate, please," you ask.

"Sure, but first let me ask you a few questions. Are you going to keep this property for a long time, or might you sell in a few years?" she inquires.

"I'm really not sure," you say.

"Well then, we can reduce your monthly payments while still allowing you to pay down that principal, which, since you want a 15-year fixed, is what you're trying to do, right?" she says.

"Yes, that's right," you reply.

"Well, I suggest a better approach. How about a 25-year fixed rate that allows you to make extra payments with no penalty? Your payments are lower, your principal can be paid down more quickly, and you have the option each month of doing either. How does that sound?"

"Sounds great!" you say.

Does this make the loan officer sound like a used car salesperson? It might, but remember, loan officers don't eat unless they sell, and if they provide you with another alternative that works in your best interest, then why not, right?

Of course, more choices can be better. But if you do get a rate quote from that loan officer with the 25-year fixed rate, you'd better get back on the phone to the other companies you've already spoken with and get their quotes on a 25-year loan.

When you change loan programs in midstream, you've lost. You're no longer in control. You must, absolutely, decide which loan program you want before you go mortgage hunting.

CONFIDENTIAL: Make Sure Your Rate Quote Covers Your Time Requirements

Another rate quote trick involves how long your rate is good for. When you get a rate quote, you're getting the rate for that very moment. If you need a rate six months from now when your new home is completed, then it's likely that this rate will no longer be available. Rates will be either up or down.

You must decide not only on the loan program, but on how long you need to guarantee, or "lock in," that rate. If your home is closing in 30 days, you'll need a 30-day quote. If it's closing in two months, you'll need a 60-day price.

The longer you extend a rate lock, the more it will cost you. For each 30-day period, it will usually cost you $1/4$ point. If you want 5.00 percent for 30 days, your loan officer might ask for $^1/_4$ point. If you want the rate for 90 days, you may be quoted "5.00 percent at 0.75 point."

What if you haven't found a house and just need a quote? If you don't watch out, you'll be fooled again. Another loan officer trick is the "today's rate" quote.

"Hi, what is your rate for a 25-year fixed-rate mortgage?"

"My rate is 3.00 percent today with no points."

"Wow!" you say. "That's great!"

"But, I can't guarantee you that rate until we have an application from you and we've received your application fee of $300. If I had your loan right now, we could get that for you," says the loan officer.

So you rush around, maybe go to the bank's web site, give the bank a check or credit card number for the $300, then call again.

"Okay, I did what you wanted. I would like to lock in that 3.00 percent rate."

"Oh, bad news. Our rates just went up. I can get you 4.00 percent right now if you'd like."

"But other lenders are quoting 3.50 percent. I want my application fee back," you protest.

"Oh, I'm sorry. Those application fees are nonrefundable; it says so on our web site and the disclosure you signed. Hey, maybe I can have the boss waive our processing fee to make it up to you. We can do that when you go to closing."

Did you follow all of that? Did you see how the borrower was led astray and now must use that lender or else lose $300? It happens all day long.

CONFIDENTIAL: "Spot" Rate Quotes Are No Good

Most lenders offer a minimum of 10- to 15-day pricing, and this is usually reserved for those loans that are already in the lender's office. Such quotes are sometimes called "spot" pricing. They're good only right then and right there. Ten days is rarely enough time to put a loan package together. It can be done, but most lenders shy away from such pressure if they have a choice.

When you make rate quote calls, some lenders will quote their 10-day price, which is usually about ⅛ point less than a 30-day price. On a $300,000 loan, ⅛ point equals $375. Other loan officers will automatically quote a 30-day price, others will be instructed to quote a 10-day price, while still others will have a choice as to what to quote.

To avoid this problem, demand a quote from all lenders for the exact period you need in order to close.

Finally, try not asking for their rate, but giving them the rate you're looking for and having them quote you. Instead of asking, "What's your 25-year rate quote for a 30-day period?" you should ask, "Can you please quote me a price on a 25-year loan, good for 30 days, at 5.50 percent?"

This is comparing exactly apples to apples. Lenders offer rates in eighths of a percent. A lender won't have just 5.00 percent or just 6.00 percent, but will offer a range in ⅛ percent increments. A lender's rate sheet will look like this:

30 year mortgage

	15 day	30 day	60 day
5.00%	2 pts	2¼ pt	2½ pt
5.125%	1.875	2.125	2.375
5.25%	1.75	2.00	2.25
5.375%	1.625	1.875	2.125
5.50%	1.50	1.75	2.00

And so on. Lenders can have rates that go as high as they can stand, but typically the lowest and the highest rates they price will be only 2.00 percentage points apart. In this case, the highest rate would be 7.00 percent, or 2.00 percentage points above the lowest rate.

Absolutely every mortgage company has a rate sheet similar to what you see here. It lists the rate, the period the rate is good for, and how much it would cost for both the rate and the time.

Now you say, "Please quote me your 30-year rate, good for 60 days, at 5.50 percent."

You have just neutralized loan officers' quoting weapons by defining the terms. When you set the quoting parameters, loan officers have less opportunity to play the shell game with you.

CONFIDENTIAL: Loan Officers May Try to Increase Their Fees to Offset a Lower Rate Quote

Let's say you were successful in getting several low quotes, and one company stood out in particular. It was $^1/_4$ point lower than its three competitors. What the loan officer didn't tell you was that it also charged a $400 processing fee and a $400 underwriting fee plus a $300 application charge.

If you had received the company's GFE along with its rate quote, you would have seen that. But if you simply called around on the telephone or e-mailed some lenders, then perhaps you wouldn't have gotten the GFE or received lender or mortgage broker closing costs.

Because you didn't ask. Unless you apply for a mortgage by completing the 1003, the loan officer is under absolutely no obligation to provide you with one, much less one that is accurate to the penny.

If you make phone calls getting rate quotes, don't forget to ask about lender or mortgage broker charges as well. Could you ask for an APR? Sure, but unless the loan officer knows how to calculate it, you could get wildly different numbers.

When getting rate quotes, ask the loan officer to include only the lender or broker fees, and not to include other fees from third parties. If you do this, you can close the loop on tricky loan quotes.

CONFIDENTIAL: You May Not Get the Rate You Were Quoted: Some Interest Rates Require a Minimum Credit Score or Have Some Other Requirement

This is not uncommon. You make various loan queries and get a good quote, only to find out later that the rate you were quoted has a prepayment penalty or requires a credit score of 800 or debt ratios below 20. Or any combination thereof.

This way, a lender can advertise certain interest rates that are designed only for the chosen few and may not be readily available to the general public for one qualification reason or another.

I recall that when I began advertising my interest rates online several years ago, certain lenders would quote rates that were $1/4$ percent lower than my absolute best offering. After several weeks of getting "beat up" in the interest-rate game, I decided to call one of these lenders, act like a consumer wanting a rate quote, and see if the rate was in fact available and how the lender was doing it.

I found out. First, there was a minimum and a maximum loan that could qualify. These levels were set so that the lender could make more money from the discount point (expressed as a percentage of the loan amount), but also were less than the then-current conforming loan limits. In other words, the range was very, very tight.

Second, there was a prepayment penalty involved. It was in effect for only a short period, two years, but it was a prepayment penalty nonetheless. And finally, a minimum credit score of 760 was needed. That's a lot of stuff: a big loan amount, but not too big, a prepayment penalty, and absolutely sterling credit.

Was this misleading? I'm not sure. As long as those conditions were outlined the very first time a consumer made a query, then I'm probably fine with it. If the consumer is quoted a super low rate, makes an application, and maybe gives the lender some money up front, then later finds out that his loan is too small or that he has to accept a prepayment penalty, then no, I'm not okay with it. It's deceiving, at best.

CONFIDENTIAL: Ultimately It's the Loan Officer Making the Rate, Not the Lender

Few mortgage companies tell their loan officers what they must quote throughout the day. Instead, loan officers are given rate sheets that show a "required" rate and point structure that the company will get. Loan officers will then mark up the interest rate, typically by anywhere from 1 to 2 points, or $^1/_4$ to $^1/_2$ percent.

Each morning, the lender sends out its interest rates for the day. These rates are not intended for consumers, but instead are to be used for rate quoting. This time, the rate sheet might look like this:

30 year mortgage

	15 day	30 day	60 day
5.00%	2 pts	$2^1/_4$ pt	$2^1/_2$ pt
5.125%	1.875	2.125	2.375
5.25%	1.75	2.00	2.25
5.375%	1.625	1.875	2.125
5.50%	1.50	1.75	2.00

The loan officer would add the company's profit on top of the points, or otherwise quote a higher rate that did not require points. The loan officer would then split whatever is added on top of the lender's rate sheet.

Some lenders have minimums that the loan officer must quote. For instance, a loan officer must make at least 100 basis points on all loans and perhaps a $300 processing fee. But anything after that is fair game. Quote whatever you have to quote to get the deal.

Conversely, some lenders also set a limit on what a loan officer can charge, say 3 points total. Anything above that amount won't be accepted. In fact, many antipredatory laws in the country stipulate how much can be charged on any particular loan.

Getting an interest-rate quote is a different breed of product. It's time-consuming, it's negotiable, and the consumer really has more influence over the final price of a mortgage than she may be aware of.

CONFIDENTIAL: You Don't Have to Pay Discount Points or Origination Fees

In fact, it's not often that paying either is a benefit to the consumer. Absolutely every lender can offer a no points, no origination fee loan. The loan officer simply increases the interest rate by enough to cover its required spread. If the required income on a loan is 100 basis points minimum, then the loan officer will quote you something like

7.00%	1 point
7.125%	¹/₂ point
7.25%	0 points

Each rate would net the lender the same amount of money, in the form of either an increased interest rate or more points. Which do you choose?

It's really easy to calculate. Simply compare the payments and the costs associated with those payments. For instance, on a $200,000 30-year loan at 6.25 percent and 1 point, your monthly payment would be $1,231, and the loan would cost you $2,000.

Now increase the rate by ¹/₄% and pay no points. The payment would be $1,264, and the loan would cost you $0.

The difference in monthly payment is $33. Take that difference and divide it into the $2,000 in points you paid, and the result is 60.6 months, or five years. It will take you five years to recover your "point cost." That's an awfully long time, in my opinion.

Yes, the $2,000 can be tax-deductible, and you're still saving that $33 each month over the life of the loan, but I suggest taking that same $2,000 and paying your principal down directly. Or you could simply keep it.

Or, you could take that $2,000 and invest it in a mutual fund or a stock, or put it aside for retirement. I've just never been a big fan of discount points or origination fees when obtaining a mortgage. I can never seem to get the numbers to work out for paying more money to get a lower rate.

CONFIDENTIAL: Rate Quotes Are Worthless Unless Your Rate Is Locked In

An interest-rate lock is an interest-rate guarantee. When you get the rate you want, you have to physically lock that in by telling your loan officer, "Please lock that in." Your loan officer will not lock you in automatically. It requires a literal request on your part.

There are various ways to lock in your rate, just as there are various lenders and protocols. There is no universal standard as to when a rate is locked in, how it's locked in, and who locks it in. Each lender can have a different method, but the effect is the same.

"I want to lock that rate in for 30 days," you say.

"Sure, I'll lock that in for you right now," says your loan officer. "I'll e-mail your lock confirmation right away."

At least, that's how it should work. When it comes to your interest rate, take no verbal guarantees. You need to get your rate lock in writing, by fax or by an e-mail confirmation. Accept no verbals.

One note: Before you get your rate lock guarantee, your loan officer must first lock that rate in with its lender's secondary department, or, if you're using a mortgage broker, the broker must contact the wholesale lender and get the rate locked in. Just because you've requested a lock from your loan officer doesn't mean that it's automatic. You're close, but it's not official.

Most locks don't require any fee if you're locking for a 30-day period. Longer lock requests might require money up front, but usually only if you're locking beyond 90 days.

Your loan officer must next lock you with his people, who will in turn confirm that request to your loan officer. It is at this point that you should get your lock confirmation from your loan officer.

I point this out because I have personally been in situations where I literally had several loans that all wanted to lock in at the same time during a very volatile period. When I was a mortgage broker, I had to complete the various lock forms by hand, fax them in, and use the time stamp on my fax request as proof of when I requested the lock.

If there was a mortgage repricing during the course of the day, and the lender raised its rates officially at, say, 2:19 p.m. PST, then the lender would honor all locks that I could prove were requested before the rate change—for example, if my time stamp had 2:16 p.m. PST. Sometimes I couldn't get all of the lock requests in fast enough. Some people got their rate locks; some did not.

Even though the buyers had told me to lock them in, those requests could not be honored until I got my confirmations from the lender. Some would get locked; some would not. Locking is a physical process, and it can take time.

Good loan officers will tell you this ahead of time—that nothing is guaranteed until the loan officer receives confirmation from either her own secondary department or her wholesale lender. Unfortunately, many loan officers will not. You could think you're locked in, all the while watching rates go up on everyone else.

If you think you're locked in, but you don't have your lock confirmation, don't take it for granted, regardless of what your loan officer tells you.

CONFIDENTIAL: Loan Officers Can Make More Money off of You Through "Market Gains"

Let's suppose you decided to go ahead and lock in your rate with your loan officer. Your loan officer said, "Sure, I'll lock you in."

But what can really happen is that you're not locked in at all. Instead, your loan officer might hold off for a few more days. Yeah, you're locked all right. You'll still get the rate you requested, but the loan officer is "floating" your request until just the right time.

Why would a loan officer float your loan request instead of locking you in right away?

It's called *market gains*. And it's done every day; you just don't know about it.

Let's compare a market gain on a mortgage to a stock purchase. Let's say you decide to buy a share of Widget stock from someone who has agreed to sell it to you for $10.00. You execute the purchase to buy that stock for $10.00 a share. But the seller knows that the stock is going down, and will continue to go down for several days. The seller then buys more shares at a still lower price, all the while making more and more money because the seller is selling at the price you agreed to—$10.00.

You're happy. You bought the stock at the price you wanted. The seller is even happier, because she made more money than she thought she would because she saw that the stock was moving and she took advantage of it.

The very same thing is done with mortgages. You can lock in a rate at 6.00 percent, your loan officer says "great!" and you may even get a lock confirmation. But if rates are moving favorably to the lender after you've locked, say they're going down toward 5.75 percent, that loan officer is making another point for each $1/4$ percent in rate that the mortgage bond markets move.

In fact, there are services that cater to loan officers who want to follow the markets this closely. Loan officers can pay for services that will broadcast live mortgage bond data to their cell phone, their BlackBerry, or their e-mail address and alert them to mortgage rate moves—the very same information that secondary departments use when deciding what rates to charge during the course of the day.

Here's an example. You lock in a $450,000 mortgage loan on a 15-year fixed rate at 5.50 percent with no points, for 30 days.

"Great!" says your loan officer. Then she goes to work.

If she follows the markets, she is constantly watching an array of charts on her computer, with mortgage bond pricing numbers scrolling across the bottom of her screen.

If the market is acting weird, or is moving in the wrong direction, she will most likely lock in your request immediately and not mess with market gains. If, however, she is watching a trend that shows mortgage bond prices moving up (lower rates, higher yield), she'll hold off on that "official" lock and make additional mortgage gains by waiting a day or two, or more.

If she locked you in immediately at the rate you requested, she could perhaps make $4,000 to $5,000 for herself and her company. But if she watched the markets, she could gain another $1/4$ to $1/2$ point . . . that's another $1,000 to $2,000 . . . that's a lot of money!

You got the rate you wanted; the loan officer made a little extra pocket change. Is this wrong? Is this an ethical issue? I'm not sure. If you wanted to lock in at 5.50 percent, your loan officer gave you a lock confirmation at 5.50 percent, and you closed at 5.50 percent, then is there a problem?

Only if you know how market gains work and you can let your loan officer know that you understand this part of the process by asking, "If I lock in this rate and rates move lower, will I get the lower rate?"

This is the question that no loan officer wants to hear, because he really can't do much about it unless he's been playing the market.

Most major mortgage companies have strict rules against market gains. And I agree with them. If a consumer wants to lock in her rate, lock in her rate. Quit goofing around trying to make a few extra bucks and go find new customers.

CONFIDENTIAL: Mortgage Brokers Can Lock You In at One Wholesale Lender, Then Lock You In at Another if Rates Move Down to Make More Money

This is a little trickier for the loan officer, because if the loan officer pulls this stunt too many times with its wholesale lenders, those lenders will cut him off completely, and soon he'll have no place to send his loans.

When an official interest rate lock is made, lenders get serious about it. Literally, when someone locks in a loan at 6.00 percent, that lender books the loan even before it closes and designates it for either sale or servicing. If a lender has $1 million to lend and suddenly five people, all with $200,000 mortgages, lock in their loans with that lender, suddenly the lender stops making mortgage loans.

At least, until the lender finds another $1 million to lend.

When loan officers "break" locks with a wholesale lender or with their secondary department, they have to answer for it. The loan officer, by locking, has officially reserved a chunk of mortgage money from the lender's accounts and taken it off of the table where other loan officers could use it.

Some mortgage brokers will officially lock in your loan with one lender, but keep an eye on mortgage rates just in case they move in her favor—and if they do, then lock with another lender, dump the old lender, and deliver to the new one. If rates move $1/4$ percent after your lock, the broker will make another point off of your loan.

While this might prove profitable to the broker for a while, she'll soon find out that some wholesale lenders don't want that sort of business. It actually costs the wholesale lender money when it has to "bust out" a lock and find another one to replace it.

CONFIDENTIAL: If Your Broker Is Playing the Market, You Could Both Lose

Market losses usually occur when you thought you were locked, but you weren't. I can't document this, but if you locked in your rate, then found out later that you weren't in fact locked, one of two things happened:

1. The loan officer made a mistake and forgot to lock you.
2. The loan officer was playing the market trying to make a few extra bucks.

Okay, let's look at scenario 1. Loan officers don't get paid unless a loan closes, so why would the loan officer forget to lock a customer's loan in, thereby guaranteeing a paycheck? Human error aside, and people do make mistakes, this can't happen that often if a loan officer wants to be a loan officer for very long.

It's very much like a professional golfer forgetting her golf clubs.

Now let's look at scenario 2. This is more likely. The problem is that some loan officers live and die by market gains. I could always tell them. Their eyes were bloodshot, they looked as if they smoked too much, and they were prematurely gray. Or bald. Or whatever.

The fact about market gains is that they can run in the opposite direction. If you thought you locked in your interest rate with Larry Loan Officer at 7.00 percent and rates have quietly moved to 7.50 percent without your knowing about it, well, there's hell to pay. And it's usually your loan officer that, in fact, does pay.

I've seen it. If a loan officer guesses wrong about market gains, it's the loan officer that has to make up the difference. Either that or he gets fired for making unauthorized market gains or losses instead of locking in the interest rate that the client originally requested.

I personally know of a loan officer that there was a running joke about: He was the only loan officer who had to bring his own checkbook to the closing table along with his clients' checkbook, because he always played the markets with his clients' interest-rate lock, and he always lost.

Loan officers who use market gains as part of their income stream are also glued to economic reports, speeches by federal officials, and worldwide political events. They subscribe to all the interest-rate services and watch the business channels all day long. They act as if they're big shots when it comes to interpreting the stock or bond markets, but in reality they're following and reacting to mortgage bond pricing.

It can get ugly. If you've locked in your mortgage rate, but you haven't received your mortgage rate lock confirmation, it's quite possible that you're not locked. If rates have moved higher since you locked in and you still don't have your confirmation, odds are that your loan officer gambled with your rate lock.

Get your lock confirmation immediately upon locking. Period.

CONFIDENTIAL: After You've Locked, Your Loan Officer Won't Tell You When Rates Have Dropped—You Have to Watch the Market Yourself

Okay, so what if you lock in and rates go the other way—down?

Not much, really. For the very same reason that, if rates go up, you don't expect a phone call from your loan officer that goes something like this:

"Hi, this is your loan officer. I know you locked and all, but rates went up, so we'd like you to consider breaking your lock and taking the new, higher rate."

Yeah, that'll happen.

But really, if rates go down, what do you do? You do have some options, but it depends upon both how far along you are in the process and how far rates have dropped.

If rates have dropped, say, $^1/_8$ percent or so, don't expect your lender to do anything at all. Tough break; you made the wrong call; let's move on with life. Even if rates have dropped $^1/_4$ percent, it's still a judgment call on what to do.

But if rates have moved more than $^1/_4$ percent, then it's time to make some moves. First, call your loan officer.

"I know rates have dropped by more than $^1/_4$ percent since I locked in. I want the lower rates," you demand.

The next thing said is from your loan officer: either "Sorry, you locked; there's nothing I can do" or "Let me see what I can do for you."

If you just ask nicely, "Hey, I was just in the neighborhood and thought you might lower my rate," then not much will happen. But if you say that if the loan officer doesn't do something about lowering the rate that you locked in, then you'll cancel the loan altogether, that gets your loan officer's attention. Big time. After all, up to this point, your loan officer has worked for you for free. Your loan hasn't closed, and might not at that, so the loan officer hasn't been paid. Talk about a waste of time.

Two things happen at this point. If you're working with a mortgage banker, the loan officer will call her secondary department and say, "Oh, no! If we don't give Mrs. Smith the new lower rate, she'll take her loan to Blue Bank!"

At this point, this is not the only call that the secondary department has received about the very same matter. In fact, depending upon how big the lender is, the phone lines are burning up with loan officers telling their sob stories: "If we don't give them the new lower market rates, well, they'll find a new lender!"

This is translated: "I'll lose my commission check!"

"If we don't give them the new rates, they'll blow their lock and not refinance with us!"

This is translated: "I'll lose my commission check!"

Secondary departments have heard it all over the years, and it all boils down to the very same thing: "Rates moved down after our company had already committed to this loan; we have to make adjustments."

Secondary departments know that they'll make adjustments on some loans; they also know that the lender will pick up new loans from other lenders that didn't adjust for their locked loans.

For every locked loan that is lost because of rates, there is another one out there from another lender that is having the very same thing happening to it. It's the loan officer's fault for not finding those loans.

That means that it's a 50/50 shot that you'll get a lower rate with your current proposed lender. If you don't, pack your bags.

Lenders also know one more thing: If you're a week or so away from your closing, regardless of what rates do, you're not going anywhere. If you try to transfer your loan, you run the risk of running out of time during the transfer and blowing your deal, losing both your earnest money and your house.

If you're a few days away from closing, you can forget about following the interest-rate market, worrying about market gains, or pulling another $1/8$ point from your loan officer. It's over. It's time to close. But don't expect a phone call from your loan officer telling you about new, lower rates. If he's doing his job properly, he's already out finding new loans.

Credit

Perhaps the single biggest change in mortgage lending involves credit and how your credit information is analyzed. Just a few years ago, your credit report was reviewed by a human being, who would pore through your credit history asking things like, "Why were you late on your student loan two years ago?" or "You went over your credit limit twice on your credit card; please explain."

In fact, loan officers would help potential borrowers craft special "explanation letters" that would answer the underwriter's question, all the while aiming for loan approval.

But automation has changed all that. Credit scoring and automated underwriting systems have changed the landscape forever.

CONFIDENTIAL: The Most Important Element in Your Loan Approval Is Your Credit Report

Everything revolves around credit—the type of loan you receive, perhaps the rate you're quoted, and even whether you get the approval you want or not. It all boils down to credit.

Your credit is defined as both your ability and your willingness to pay back your creditors. Ability means that you can afford to pay back your creditors, and willingness means that you have the inclination to do so. Both components need to be present to establish a good positive credit history.

How do you get a history? Businesses that you borrow from send your payment patterns to a great big centralized database. Actually, there are three great big centralized databases; they're called Equifax, Trans-Union and Experian.

Businesses that extend credit to consumers pay money to access these databases as well as putting consumer payment information into them. If you pay Widget Factory on time every month, then Widget Factory sends those payment patterns to the various databases.

If you apply to another company for credit, that company will tap one of those databases with your name, your social security number, and other personal data about you and review how you've paid other businesses. If the company's credit extension guidelines match what you want from it, then, voilà, you've got a new credit account.

CONFIDENTIAL: You May Have Mistakes on Your Credit Report That You Don't Know About

You have to ask. The three credit bureaus simply collect data and report them back when asked. You can have mistakes on a credit report and not know about it, and this can damage your credit file.

There is no requirement that credit bureaus tell you about errors. In fact, credit bureaus don't know whether something in your credit report is a mistake or not; they just spit out what's been given to them. If you paid a credit card $100 and the credit bureau states that you paid only $10, it's not the credit bureau's fault. It's usually the credit card company that transposed a decimal somewhere.

But you'll never know about these mistakes unless you ask the credit bureaus directly. You do this by getting copies of your credit report from all three bureaus and reviewing them for mistakes. When you find a mistake, you contact the credit bureau and inform it of the error.

When you've established that there is an error, the bureau is then required to contact the other two bureaus and have them clean up the mistake as well. But it's your job to look for mistakes, not the bureaus'.

Recent changes in credit-reporting laws now make it easier for you to get your credit reports. All you have to do is visit www.annualcreditreport .com, where you can get your report from all three bureaus at no cost to you.

If you do find errors, and you can document the mistakes, once you provide that documentation to one bureau, it's not necessary for you to contact the other two as well to make sure they get the corrected information. The law requires one bureau to notify the other bureaus when a mistake is found and corrected.

CONFIDENTIAL: Writing an Explanation Letter to the Credit Bureau Does Absolutely No Good

A consumer has the right to include an explanation letter in a credit report. For instance, if there's a late payment on a credit account and you find out about it when you review your credit report, you need to find out if the late payment was, in fact, late.

You find the old statement from the creditor, find the copy of the cancelled check or online payment, make copies, and send them to the credit bureau. If the negative information is a mistake, the information should be removed completely from the report.

But if it's not a mistake, you have the right to prepare a letter that must be included with your credit file.

Let's say that, yes, you were late, but there were extenuating circumstances. You did make the payment on time, but for some reason the payment never arrived at the creditor's payment center.

Soon, you received a late payment warning in the mail from the creditor, so you called the creditor and said, "I mailed that payment two weeks ago," or whatever.

The creditor then said, "Yes, we received it; don't worry."

But the check still didn't clear. At least, it didn't clear for a couple of months, but finally it did. So you called the creditor, and the person on the phone told you that the creditor had received it, but it was never reflected that way. When you review your credit report and see the error, you try to correct it by calling the creditor.

The creditor replies, "We don't show any record of its being made on time; in fact, we show that it was two months late."

You're astonished. You say, "But when I called you, you said that you had the payment and not to worry! Now it's showing up late on my credit report!"

"I'm sorry," replies the creditor. "I don't know who you talked to back then . . ."

"Fred!" you say.

"I'm sorry, but Fred doesn't work here anymore. There's nothing I can do," the creditor finally says.

You're heartbroken. But wait! You have the right to include a letter with your credit file explaining your side of the story, don't you? Of course you do. So you compose a great letter, with as many facts as you can remember, and send it to the credit bureau.

Guess what? Nobody cares. Several years ago, lenders read credit explanation letters when they were included in the file: "I bought this piece of junk from them and it never worked, so I didn't pay them!" or "I was out of the country for three months," or "I moved and they never sent the bill to my new address."

Whatever the case, letters were read by underwriters who were deciding whether or not to approve a particular mortgage. But not now. With the advent of credit scoring, credit explanation letters have gone the way of the dinosaur. If a friend or acquaintance or real estate agent suggests writing a letter to the bureau explaining your side of the story, you're wasting your time with regard to a mortgage.

CONFIDENTIAL: If There's a Mistake on Your Credit Report, It's Your Lender Who Can Best Help You Fix It, Not the Bureau

You didn't know that, did you? You didn't think your lender would help you fix your credit report? Well, it's not exactly the lender; it's your loan officer who is your best friend when it comes to fixing errors.

Remember that your loan officer doesn't get paid unless your loan closes. If there's a mistake on your credit report that's lowering your credit score or otherwise blocking your AUS approval, your loan officer has some contacts that you don't have.

Credit-reporting agencies solicit lenders' business every single day. They hire sales reps, just like many other businesses, to make sales calls. No matter what lender or mortgage broker you end up using, there's a credit-reporting agency representative who is paid to get business from that lender or broker.

These agencies are not direct employees of the three major credit bureaus; they are employees of companies that pull data from these bureaus and report and provide those data to lenders who want to issue credit decisions for their consumers as part of their business or trade.

These sales reps promise things such as lower prices for reports, timely reporting, and finally assistance when there are problems. Fixing mistakes on credit reports is where these companies earn their keep—and it's your loan officer who knows them. Forget about credit explanation letters—your loan officer can fix this for you.

If it's a mistake.

What's a mistake in the world of credit reporting? A mistake is something that can be proven wrong by third-party sources. Did the creditor say you were late on one of your payments to it? You can't simply tell your loan officer, "No, that's not correct"; instead, you will have to provide your loan officer with third-party documentation verifying that what you say is correct.

Find that cancelled check and get a copy of that old statement, give it to your loan officer, and have her take a look at it. If in fact you can show that what was due was paid on time, through a date cancellation on the back of your check, or show how the account was paid online, then all your loan officer has to do is show that documentation to the credit agency sales rep and he will wipe it clean—something that can take months when consumers try to do it by themselves.

Credit agency sales reps get paid to do things like this, and your loan officer has a vested interest in getting mistakes fixed and fixed fast.

CONFIDENTIAL: Underwriters Don't Look at Your Various Credit Accounts and See How Many Late Payments You Have or Haven't Made

Underwriters rarely even review a credit report. They don't have to. When an automated underwriting system, or AUS, approval is issued, a credit report is redundant. The AUS will pull a credit score while at the same time locating any public records such as bankruptcy filings or tax liens.

Loan officers don't automatically run credit reports any longer; instead, they go directly to the AUS for a decision. Just a few years ago, the underwriter would indeed not just glance at but pore over a credit report, looking to see if any late payments were made, when they were made, and how often. Not so now.

Automated underwriting systems have close to eliminated most credit report reviews by humans. Do you need good credit? Of course you do, but it's simply reviewed differently.

CONFIDENTIAL: Bankruptcy Doesn't Automatically Mean that You Can't Get a Mortgage

This is a common misunderstanding. This credit myth is so pervasive that it still keeps qualified people from applying for a home loan at all.

The biggest bankruptcy myth is that one can't get a mortgage until seven years have passed. Wrong. In fact, loans can be issued to those with bankruptcies even if their bankruptcy is just one day old. There are loans available for those with good credit and for those with not good credit. And both loan types make allowances for bankruptcies. If you've got a bankruptcy in your long ago or recent past, take heart; you can still buy.

Conventional and government lending issued under Fannie Mae, Freddie Mac, FHA, or VA guidelines allow for such instances. But there are certain bankruptcy rules for each.

Fannie Mae and Freddie Mac loans typically can give a loan approval if the bankruptcy is only 48 months old. Government programs can make a loan when bankruptcies are only two years old.

Each set of guidelines asks that after a bankruptcy has been discharged, credit has been reestablished through other credit accounts, such as a credit card or car loan. And as for those who think creditors don't issue credit to people who have experienced a bankruptcy, they're wrong. There's a huge industry designed specifically for those who need to reestablish good credit. Yeah, rates are a little higher under these circumstances, but that's to be expected.

Under any circumstances, always try for a conventional or government loan first.

CONFIDENTIAL: Conventional Lenders Can Make a Loan Even if the Bankruptcy Is Less Than Four Years Old

In this case, a mortgage can be issued when it can be demonstrated that the bankruptcy was caused by extreme circumstances, most specifically by the death of the "breadwinner."

The first time I experienced this was many years ago, when I was a mortgage broker in San Diego. I got a call from a woman whose husband had just died. She was trying to buy the house they were renting, but she was told that because of her bankruptcy, she would have to wait four years before she could buy the home.

She had been a stay-at-home mom, and her husband had died unexpectedly. She was an attorney who hadn't practiced for a few years, but she got a new job at a law firm in her town. Time and time again she was told that because of her bankruptcy, which had been made necessary by the death of her husband, she could not get a home loan.

That information was wrong. She could buy a home. Unfortunately, she had contacted too many loan officers who simply didn't know any better. She found me, we documented her story (she even had to supply a copy of her husband's death certificate), and she bought her home. This is still one of my best memories in home lending.

CONFIDENTIAL: If You're in a Chapter 13 Bankruptcy, You Can Still Get a Mortgage Through FHA

FHA loans make allowances for this. If you're currently in a Chapter 13 bankruptcy, FHA may still let you qualify for a mortgage. Its guidelines require that the bankruptcy payments are being made on a timely basis and that the bankruptcy trustee gives you permission to buy the home. I don't have any official statistics on how often FHA will make such exceptions, but I can say that I've never seen a home purchase request be denied when the Chapter 13 repayments have been made on time.

CONFIDENTIAL: Mortgage Lenders Make No Distinction Between a Chapter 7 and a Chapter 13

There are currently two types of personal bankruptcy filings, those filed under Bankruptcy Code Chapters 7 and 13. Chapter 7 is a complete discharge of all debts that qualify. Chapter 13 is a reorganization of those debts into a monthly repayment plan that ultimately repays the consumers' debtors, typically under renegotiated payment terms.

Lenders can make a bankruptcy allowance based upon when a bankruptcy was actually discharged. When a lender wants to see a certain period of time elapse before a loan can be issued, the lender looks at the discharge date. In a Chapter 7 bankruptcy, which removes all debt, the date is set on the discharge date of the bankruptcy, not the filing date.

The discharge date on a Chapter 13, on the other hand, is established when the repayment plan has been completed. If the Chapter 13 took two years to pay everyone back, then the date is established after the two years has passed. If a loan requires four years since the bankruptcy discharge and it took two years to pay off the Chapter 13, then it will require a total of six years. If instead a Chapter 7 was filed and discharged and the requirement was four years, then the loan will require only four years.

Don't confuse that notion with the idea that there is no credit review whatsoever. There is. But it's the advent of credit scoring that has made manual reviews mostly unnecessary.

Credit scoring for mortgages is a relatively new aspect of mortgage lending. Scoring has been around for a long, long time. It used to be done manually by underwriters. But now, numbers are assigned to an applicant's credit report, with a higher number reflecting better credit and a lower number reflecting worse credit.

These scores are commonly called FICO scores because the method of to calculating them was developed by a company called Fair Isaac Corporation, or FICO. FICO scores can range from 350 to 850, with the average consumer credit score being around 680.

CONFIDENTIAL: Conventional and Government Loans Don't Require a Minimum Credit Score

With all the hoopla about credit scoring, consumers have been given a false impression about credit scoring in general. You'll hear "Don't lower your score!" or "You'd better find out what your score is before you apply for a mortgage!" or some such claim. True, it's important to know where you stand creditwise, and your FICO number is an indicator, but let's not get carried away here.

When you apply for a conventional or government loan product, you won't get approved or declined because of a number. There may be certain "boutique" or "specialty" loan programs that require minimum scores, such as certain zero percent financing loans, but in general, a specific score is not a requirement. Decent credit? Sure. A particular number? No.

A credit score is an analytical number that attempts to predict the likelihood of default on a loan. It reflects your credit and payment patterns over the most recent two-year period. Someone can have excellent credit over the years, with scores in the 800s, and then have something bad happen, like the loss of a job, illness, or some other financial disaster. After a few months of late payments, charging over credit limits, or collection accounts, scores can plummet quickly.

At the same time, someone can have terrible credit over the years, then finally wake up and smell the credit coffee and concentrate on improving his credit score. After about 24 months of credit diligence, paying off collection items, reducing credit balances, and making payments on time, he'll find that his scores can compete with some of the best around.

CONFIDENTIAL: Scores Are Combined with Other Risk Elements; Credit Is Paramount, but It Is Not the Only Issue

Scores are just part of the picture, not all of it. And just because you have a higher score than your neighbor doesn't automatically mean that you're going to get a lower rate. Other things are factored in when issuing a loan approval—other things such as the amount of the down payment compared to the sales price of the home, debt ratios, and assets are all in play.

I can recall looking at two different loan applications on my desk. Both were for refinancing their current mortgage. Both wanted a 30-year fixed-rate loan, but their credit scores were far from the same. One guy had a score of 580, and the other had a score above 750. They both got my best rates.

Unfortunately, there is simply so much misinformation about scores that one would automatically think that the guy with 580 wouldn't even be approved for the mortgage refinancing, much less worry about what rate he would get. One prominent web site flat-out makes the incorrect claim that if your score falls into this or that range, that will determine your rate. Of course, this information comes from a company that tries to sell consumers credit-reporting tools, books, and services.

The information states, for example, that if your score is between 760 and 850, then your rate would be about 6.00 percent. But if your score falls between 639 and 620, then your rate would zoom to 7.62 percent. Unfortunately, this false information comes from perhaps one of the most prominent credit information companies.

The web site also implies, since its score chart doesn't go below 620, that if your score is, say, 580, then forget about it, pal. Nothing could be further from the truth. It's obvious that this site doesn't do mortgage loans, but it could be stopping people from applying.

The guys with the 580 and 760 scores? They looked like this:

	580 Score	760 Score
Loan amount	$ 185,000	$220,000
Value of home	$650,000	$ 250,000
Housing debt ratio	19	45

Using bad information, assuming that Mr. 580 could even qualify for a mortgage, he would be handed an interest rate closer to 8.00 percent and the more handsome Mr. 760 would get the coveted, lowest rate on the planet, 6.00 percent.

That's not so, and it didn't happen. They both got the same, lowest rate. Why? Is it unfair that the guy with 760 was handed the same rate as the guy with 580? Remember, there are factors in a loan approval other than score.

In this case, Mr. 580 had lots of equity in his home, while Mr. 760 did not. Mr. 580 had his housing debt ratio in the teens; Mr. 760 did not. After the AUS evaluated both loans, they were approved under the very same terms.

On the other hand, if Mr. 580 hadn't had all the equity, his loan balance had been very near his home value, and his ratios had been as high as Mr. 760's, then it's not likely that Mr. 580 would have been approved.

Scores are one only one item considered during a loan approval; they're not the only thing.

CONFIDENTIAL: While There May Be Three Different Credit Scores, the Lender Always Uses the Middle One

The three credit bureaus all use the same FICO credit-scoring model, although they all call them by different names (go figure, right?), but they will almost always have different numbers. How can that be if they use the same algorithms? Easy. They have different data.

Each bureau resides in a different geographic area and gathers different data at different intervals. Local merchants may report credit information to their local bureau, but may not report it to others. Or information that is reported to one bureau may take some time to show up at another one. Since the length of time a particular item is reported is part of a score, if a late payment is reported earlier by one bureau, but isn't picked up until some time later by another, then those two scores will be different.

No, lenders don't average them together. To compensate for these variances, lenders won't take your best score (rats!); they will throw away your lowest score (yea!) and use the one in the middle. It's the middle score that most probably reflects your payment patterns.

CONFIDENTIAL: If You're Applying with Someone Else on a Mortgage Loan, the Lender Will Use the Credit Score of the Person That Makes the Most Money

Fair or not fair, that's how it works. A common example might be a couple where the wife makes $100,000 a year as an attorney and the husband makes $50,000 as an accountant. If the wife has a credit score of 550 and the husband has excellent credit with a 810 credit score, then the lender will use the 550 score.

No, they don't average them together and get 680. The credit score used for loan approval purposes will be the lower one, 550.

It doesn't matter if you are a married couple or not. What if everyone on the application makes the same money? They use the lower score. It's a toss-up in this case, but lenders will still use the lower score.

CONFIDENTIAL: A Cosigner Can't Erase Someone Else's Bad Credit

This is a common misconception. "Hello, Blue Bank, I have bad credit, but my uncle has great credit, and he's willing to cosign." So what?

While having a cosigner can certainly help in some cases, it doesn't help with credit issues. Having a cosigner can help when more income is needed to qualify for the loan or when the down payment is coming primarily from the cosigner.

But if the elephant in the room is the borrower's terrible credit, the nice uncle can't do anything about that.

CONFIDENTIAL: It's Better to Remove an Extra Person on a Loan Application if That Person Has Bad Credit.

When you are buying with someone else and that someone else has shaky credit, it's not a requirement that you put that person on the mortgage. The mortgage is simply a note that the borrower pays back using the home as collateral.

Ownership of the property is designated by the title report. All owners of the property will appear on a document called the deed. The deed and the loan are two different things. If the borrower with good credit can get approved without using the other person's income, then take the person with bad credit off of the mortgage application altogether.

The person with bad credit will still have ownership, evidenced by his or her name on the deed, but won't appear on the loan.

CONFIDENTIAL: Paying Off and Closing Credit Accounts Will Hurt Your Credit

Those of you who have had credit for several years will probably shake your heads at this. But it's true. Paying off and closing credit accounts will actually harm your credit score, not help it.

From an overall credit perspective, it makes sense to close out accounts that you don't use anymore. It makes sense to me. Why keep them if you don't need them? It's possible that someone could steal your identity and use those accounts, or you could have an old balance and not know it, or, well, it's just a prudent thing to close them down.

But from a credit score standpoint, that's a mistake. No one knows, except Fair Isaac, of course, exactly how credit scores are calculated, and FICO plans to keep it that way to avoid abuse. But there are certain things that are known about credit scores that can provide some clues as to how to improve your credit score and what constitutes a score.

The two most important factors in your score are your payment history and the amounts owed.

Your payment history shows your ability and willingness to pay your creditors back when you're supposed to; it accounts for about 35 percent of your total credit score. Each month, when you get a credit card statement, you'll see your credit limit, your balance, your minimum payment due, and the due date.

You may have a $10,000 credit card limit and owe $5,000, and your minimum monthly payment might be $125, due on the 24th of the month. All of these factors affect your credit score. Make your payments on time, at least pay the minimum, and don't go over your credit limit. If you do these things, then you've just taken care of more than one-third of how your score will be figured.

CONFIDENTIAL: It's Not Whether the Payment Was Late, It's *How* Late It Was That Makes the Difference

If your payment arrives at the lender on the 25th and not the 24th, don't sweat it—at least from a credit score basis. The terms of most credit cards allow the lender to begin charging you higher rates if your payments don't arrive before the due date. But if something happened and your payment arrives late, don't worry, as long as your payment is not more than 30 days past the due date.

It's this 30-day period that credit companies report, and what will hurt your score is if you pay more than 30 days past the due date. The next bad date is 60 days past the due date, then 90 days, then 120 days, and then probably right into a collection account.

You should be concerned that you get your payments in before the due date to preserve your credit card interest rate, but if something happens and you don't make it, make sure you get the payment to the creditor before 30 days past the due date or it will be reported as a negative item in your report.

And it's this payment pattern that can whack your score if you have late payments, because your payment history constitutes 35 percent of your total score. Mess up here and you've got some serious cleaning up to do.

CONFIDENTIAL: To Optimize Your Credit Score, You Should Have a Balance of About One-Third of Your Credit Limit

The next most important item in score calculation takes into consideration your amounts owed, which accounts for about 30 percent of your total credit score. Your balances are viewed in relation to your credit limit, both whether you've ever gone over your credit limit (which hurts your score) and how much credit you have available to you at any given time. Lenders like to see an ideal balance of about one-third of your total credit limits. Limiting your total balances to 30 percent of your available balances will markedly improve your score.

Notice that I didn't say anything about paying off credit balances. The magic number is 30 percent. Not 0 percent. If you want to optimize your credit score, then you need to have both available credit and balances. The old credit adage of canceling old accounts can hurt you, not help you. How's that?

Let's say you have three credit accounts, all with equal credit lines, adding up to a $10,000 limit. Now let's say you have a $3,000 balance on one card and zero balances on the other two. You're at the magical 30 percent ratio: $3,000 is 30 percent of $10,000. The longer you keep this approximate percentage, the more your score will improve. And improve and improve.

If you pay off the $3,000 entirely and have a 0 percent balance, your score could actually be damaged. I'm not kidding. The theory is that having balances shows an ability and a willingness to pay on time. With no balances, how can you demonstrate that you can pay on time? When you think of it that way, it makes sense.

Why is the ratio about one-third of balances owed to credit limits? Over the years, FICO has developed historical data that indicate that those with the best credit histories had credit available to them, used it, and paid it back.

A credit card company doesn't want you to *have* its credit card. It wants you to *use* its credit card to buy things with. You'll borrow money from the company and pay it back with interest.

Now take those same three credit cards, and cancel one of them. Now your credit limit is about $6,000, and your balance is still $3,000. Ouch. Your ratio now is 50 percent. You owe $3,000, and your limit is $6,000. This pattern can indicate a propensity to borrow too much money, potentially getting you into trouble. The longer you keep this ratio at 50 percent, the more your credit score will slowly erode.

Cancel one more card? Now you have a $3,000 balance along with a $3,000 credit limit. You're at 100 percent. Your score will take a beating. It doesn't matter if you've paid that account on time or not. That pattern will be reflected in the payment history calculation. If you're at 100 percent, regardless of whether you've paid on time or not, your scores will drop and drop fast.

On the other hand, if you now know where 65 percent of your score comes from, you can take steps to adjust those factors. You'll find that if you take care of these two things, payment history and amounts owed, everything else will take care of itself.

But what if you want to buy now and your credit is damaged? Are you out of luck? No, there's another category of lending called subprime lending designed for those who have bad credit.

CONFIDENTIAL: Subprime Lending Is Not a Bad Thing

A common misunderstanding about subprime loans is that they're made by loan sharks who charge sky-high rates and take advantage of someone's poor credit situation. While there are loan sharks in the world, a subprime loan is not automatically a bad thing. Just ask those who were granted a second chance at credit and are now living in their new homes.

Loans designed for those with hurt credit can be found at almost every mortgage lender in the country, be it a mortgage broker or a mortgage banker. Every national lender that you see advertising on television has a subprime division. The difference is that these lenders will separate these two divisions into separate business units.

If you apply at a lender and get declined because of your credit, ask the loan officer to rerun your application to get a subprime offering. It's possible that your loan officer will resubmit your loan application right then and there, but often your application is handed off to a different loan officer and probably to another location entirely. It's the same company, but a different division.

CONFIDENTIAL: Don't Go to Lenders Who "Specialize in Helping People with Bad Credit"

At least, don't go to them until you've tried regular lenders. Because of the Internet, everyone's smart. At least, they think they are, because anytime someone has a question about anything, he simply Googles it and goes on about his business. While that's fine for looking up a stock price from yesterday or getting baseball scores from 10 years back, it's dangerous in the world of mortgage lending.

There is simply too much bad information out there, and when it comes to self-evaluation of credit, consumers can automatically take the low credit road when they don't have to. Remember Mr. 580? Had he relied only on information culled from various web sites, he might not have applied at his bank. He might have applied directly with a lender or mortgage broker that "specialized" in "helping" people with damaged credit.

Don't make that mistake. If you think you have bad credit, the lender will tell you what's bad and what's not bad.

CONFIDENTIAL: Unlike Conventional and Government Loans, Subprime Loans Have Strict Credit Score Requirements

Subprime mortgage loans are a different animal in many respects, with the most striking difference being the conformity to lending guidelines. If a loan requires a score of 600 to be approved, you'll need to have a 600 score. Period. Or else you'll have to rearrange your credit request.

Subprime lending exists because damaged credit exists. There is a market for it. People who have bad credit don't like the fact that they have bad credit and want to do something to fix it, and one of the best ways to do that is to buy a house and begin reestablishing a credit history.

Subprime loans will have higher rates than loans reserved for people with good credit. How much higher? Not a lot higher, but higher nonetheless. If someone with good credit can get a rate of 7.00 percent, then an equivalent subprime rate for someone with outstanding collection accounts, late payments, and maybe some defaulted student loans could be 3.00 percent higher, or 10 percent.

Some decry this rate as usurious and in bad taste. They feel that it's taking advantage of someone when he's down by making his house payments higher. However, there's a higher risk in lending money to people who have negative credit than in lending to someone with excellent credit. To offset that increase in risk, lenders will ask for a higher rate.

In the not too distant past, those with bad credit were simply locked out of home ownership altogether, never having the opportunity to rebuild their credit profile because no one would give them a second or even a third chance.

Those who frown on the subprime mortgage industry don't fully understand what's at issue. Subprime lenders get people into homes who otherwise would continue renting.

But there are no corners to cut in subprime lending. If a loan requires a 580 score and the loan applicant's score is 579, then no loan. Or the applicant has to compensate by putting more money down, buying a smaller home, reducing their debt ratios, or any combination of those three.

CONFIDENTIAL: Subprime Loans Are Designed for Short-Term Use

If you think of a subprime loan as a Band-Aid or a temporary credit solution, then you understand subprime lending's place in the mortgage business. Yes, there are 30-year fixed-rate subprime loans, but if you're shopping for a subprime loan and aren't really in the mood to pay higher rates for the rest of your mortgage life, then long-term fixed-rate loans aren't for you.

Nor should they be for anybody. Instead, opt for shorter-term loans called hybrids. A hybrid is an adjustable-rate mortgage that is fixed for a shorter term, such as three or five years. The reason to choose a hybrid is that the rates are lower than for subprime fixed-rate loans, and you plan on refinancing anyway when your credit scores get better.

Hybrids are typically 1 to 2 percent lower than fixed-rate fare. So instead of getting a 10 percent rate, you could get 8.00 percent or better with a hybrid program.

Being short-term also means not paying discount points or origination fees. If you're getting a subprime loan, demand a loan program without those charges. They're out there; every lender offers them. If you find a loan officer who claims otherwise, go somewhere else.

CONFIDENTIAL: All Lenders Follow the Same Subprime Underwriting Guidelines

Subprime lending, like other mortgage lending, also has certain lending characteristics that allow lenders to buy and sell mortgage loans, just as they do with conventional and government mortgages. There may be slight variations within loan guidelines, but overall, subprime loans follow the very same road.

That means that a subprime loan at one lender is underwritten according to the same standards as a subprime loan at another lender down the street. When you see advertisements screaming, "We offer loans for people with bad credit!" don't think the lender that is advertising is different from any other. It's not.

There are mortgage firms that specialize in subprime lending, just as other lenders can specialize in construction loans or FHA mortgages. But the fact that a lender claims that subprime lending is all it does doesn't mean that it has something that no one else has. It doesn't. That loan is underwritten the same way no matter where the loan goes.

Subprime loans are categorized, usually by a letter grade. The best subprime rates might be reserved for A- borrowers. The next lowest grade would be B, then C, then sometimes D.

Other lenders take those same credit grades and adjust them to reflect a B+ or a B- or some such variation. Again, this isn't something that's unique to that lender or mortgage broker; it's nothing more than a marketing gimmick, to try to make that lender appear different from the other ones.

Subprime mortgages are a commodity, just like conventional loans are.

CONFIDENTIAL: Loans by Themselves Aren't Necessarily Predatory, but a Loan Officer Can Make a Predatory Loan

Mortgage loans are not made just to foreclose on someone. If the lender makes a loan, then forecloses, something has gone very wrong. Foreclosing is an expensive, long-drawn-out process. Some states require lenders to go to court, in front of a judge, to get their collateral back. Other states have other methods. Whatever method is used to recover the home, a foreclosure is bad news all around.

The origin of the mortgage term *predatory* is hard to pin down, but the term has made headlines over the previous few years. A predatory loan, by loose definition, is one designed to take advantage of a homeowner by pressuring her to take a loan that she doesn't want or need, stripping equity from the borrower with continuous refinancing, or charging high fees during the course of a loan closing.

I say by loose definition, because there is no universal, state-to-state, definition of a predatory loan. Various state laws have been enacted to protect the consumer from predatory lenders. But loans aren't designed with the intent to foreclose. Loans are designed to be paid back, or the lender won't be a lender for very long. Lending and foreclosing don't belong together.

Thus, loans themselves aren't predatory. It's the greedy, no-good loan officer who makes a loan predatory by charging high fees and stripping equity. There's a big difference between the loan officer's interest and the ultimate lender's interest.

A loan officer makes money when the loan closes. And that's it. Move on to the next loan. A lender makes money on that same loan when it collects interest each month or sells the loan to another lender, who will also make money every month. A loan officer may concentrate only on closing that one deal, making as much as he possibly can on it, and then finding someone else to prey on.

I remember a telephone call I got one day from a lady who said that she wasn't happy with the mortgage company she was working with to close her deal. At the time, a 30-year mortgage rate could be found in most places at around 6.50 percent. But she was being quoted closer to 7.00 percent and was also being charged 3 points because her loan officer said that her credit score was pushing up her rate.

I discussed her situation with her, and I couldn't figure out why she was being charged such a high rate and so many points. I could guess that the loan officer was trying to shaft her with all those points, but the rate didn't match either. The only thing I could do was take a loan application from her, run it through the AUS, and see what came up. But, again from what she told me, she shouldn't have been given such rotten terms.

Her loan went through the AUS, and in just a few moments I got her approval for an everyday 30-year fixed-rate loan at around 6.50 percent, without any points or origination fees. The loan officer she had been working with was simply trying to take advantage of an old lady, and was probably making close to 5 points total on her when you figured in the higher rate.

The loan officer took a regular loan and made it predatory. The loan wasn't a subprime loan; it had nothing to do with credit. The loan officer was simply trying to take advantage of this lady to the tune of about $7,500.

There are bad loans out there, or at least loans that are constructed to be bad by the loan officer. How do you know if a loan is predatory? If you're getting charged anything above 2 discount points on any loan, I'd:

Question it

Shop it

If you're getting quoted 4 points plus several hundred dollars in lender fees, just ask the loan officer, "Pardon me, is this loan considered predatory?" Asking that question will raise several red flags with the loan officer. First, the loan officer will be surprised that you even know to ask the question, and second, it will also make the loan officer think he's about to get turned into the authorities.

Shop it by calling other lenders in the area and getting quotes from them. Make a few phone calls, tell the loan officer that you've applied for a mortgage with Red Bank, you have a credit score of 550, have 20 percent down, and your debt ratios are below 50. Or whatever your approval terms are. Competing loan officers most likely have the exact same loan program. They might call it something different, but it's still probably identical to the one you're being screwed on down the street.

CONFIDENTIAL: Subprime Loans Aren't Harder to Get Approved

They're approved just like any other loan. I've heard people claim that just because a loan is subprime, the loan officer does more work to get the loan approved. Nonsense. I've closed my fair share of subprime loans, and it takes no more work than any other loan.

Just as conventional loans and government loans can be approved as long as their approval guidelines are met, subprime mortgage loans are approved in a similar fashion.

Almost every major subprime lender uses an AUS. A loan officer will input your 1003 into the AUS, wait a few moments, and receive the approval. The approval will spell out exactly what is needed to fund the loan.

Nothing more and nothing less. There are some loan officers who will make it appear that they've been burning the midnight oil trying to get your loan approved, but that's not the case.

Nor has your loan officer spent hours and hours on the phone arguing with an underwriter or trying to convince a lender to give you one more shot at life. Nope, the AUS will not only spell out just what is required to close your loan application, but also run your credit report, pull some scores, and offer you an array of loan options from which to choose.

It's not rocket science, but some loan officers may try to make it look that way. They'll try to make it appear difficult so that they can charge you more points. I've even read so-called experts telling consumers that the reason subprime loans cost more is because the loan officer works harder on them. It's simply not true.

Loan Choices

I worked for several years in the mortgage lending division of a major bank, and each day the bank's secondary department would distribute its daily rate sheets—all eight pages of them, with each page having about 15 different loan programs with different available rates. That's a lot of loan programs—in fact, a little too many, in my opinion. But in the world of marketing, it's all about distinguishing yourself.

CONFIDENTIAL: There Are Really Only Two Types of Loan: Fixed and Adjustable

That's it. There's not a lot more to it other than lenders offering different variations on a fixed-rate loan and an adjustable-rate loan. Fixed-rate loans can have terms as short as 10 years or all the way out to 40 years—or longer.

Adjustable-rate mortgages, on the other hand, can be based on a variety of indexes, some of which you may have heard of and some not. Adjustable rates are set using an index and a margin. There is a third category of loan program called a hybrid, but it's really not all that different.

A hybrid is actually an adjustable-rate mortgage with special terms attached.

The rates on adjustable-rate mortgages, or ARMs, can change. That's why they're called adjustable. Fortunately, however, you're aware of what those changes can be. An ARM is first based upon an index, the starting point for how your monthly payments will be calculated.

The most common indexes are the one-year Treasury index and LIBOR.

The Treasury index is the one-year Treasury note issued by the U.S. government. LIBOR stands for London Interbank Offered Rate; it is similar to our fed funds and discount rates.

Next, the margin is added to the index to give the interest rate on which the consumer's mortgage payment is based.

If the index is 4.5 and the margin is 2.75, then the interest rate would adjust to 4.5 + 2.75, or 7.25 percent. This is also called the fully indexed rate. On a loan amount of $200,000, the monthly payment would be $1,364.

When do ARMs adjust? At predetermined adjustment periods, most usually every six months or one year. Whichever adjustment period is used, you'll know about it, as it's included in the terms of your original note.

A one-year adjustable will typically adjust once per year, a six-month ARM will adjust every six months, and monthly ARMs will adjust, well, monthly.

CONFIDENTIAL: Rate Caps Protect You When You Have an ARM—Pay Attention to Your Caps and Make Sure Your ARM Has Them

There are consumer protections that are built into ARMs, and they're called caps. There are adjustment caps and lifetime caps. These caps are also spelled out in your original note.

Caps protect the consumer from wild rate swings, while also protecting the lender from having to foreclose on a property because the consumer suddenly can't afford the payments any longer.

Let's say you have a neat little 5.50 percent ARM that is based on the one-year Treasury. At your anniversary date, your lender will take the then-current one-year Treasury index as reported by the federal government. Let's say that index is 5.00 percent. The lender will add that index to your margin of 2.50 percent to arrive at your fully indexed rate of 7.50 percent. Your new monthly payments will be based upon 7.50 percent until your next adjustment period.

But wait. Let's try another example. At your one-year anniversary, the one-year Treasury index is 10.00 percent, not 5.00 percent. Now add your margin and your fully indexed rate is 12.50 percent.

Yikes! Your $200,000 mortgage loan payment has gone from $1,135 to $2,134! It's doubled! You can't afford your home any longer!

But thanks to adjustment caps, in any single adjustment, the rate can't increase more than 2 percent above your starting rate. No matter what rates do, you're protected, even if they go into the 20.00 percent range as they did in the late 1980s. Instead of going to 12.50 percent, your rate is capped at 2 percent above 5.50 percent, or 7.50 percent. Now your payment has gone up to $1,398. That's higher, but it's nothing like $2,134.

Another cap on ARMs is the lifetime cap, or the maximum that your rate can ever be throughout the life of your loan. Common interest-rate caps are 6.00 percent above your starting rate, although most government ARMs and some conventional ARMs have 5.00 percent caps. If you started at 5.50 percent and you have a 5 percent lifetime cap, your rate can never, ever be higher than 5.50 percent plus 5.00 percent, or 10.50 percent.

CONFIDENTIAL: Subprime Loans Have Significantly Higher Caps and Margins

Common adjustment caps for subprime ARMs can be 5 percent or more higher than the start rate. Forget about the annual cap adjustment and the lifetime cap. At the first adjustment period, subprime ARMs can actually go straight to their lifetime cap.

In this case, if your lifetime cap is 5 percent, then your margin may also be 5 percent. So no matter what you originally started out at, when you adjust, it's likely that your mortgage payment will increase considerably.

That's also why, when you secure a subprime loan, it's important that you make it your life's work to rebuild your credit during your initial loan term to avoid these huge payment swings.

CONFIDENTIAL: When Comparing ARMs from Different Lenders, Pay Close Attention to the Starting Rate

The starting rate is often called the "teaser" because it starts out artificially low, lower than the fully indexed rate. A teaser, or starting rate, is the rate you get at the very beginning of your ARM loan. A teaser could be at 4.00 percent, for example, just to get you "in the door," while the fully indexed rate might be 6.00 percent or more.

You can't compare teaser rates from one lender to the next; they won't be there the following year. Both lenders, if they base their one-year ARM on the same index, will take that very same index and add the margin to arrive at the new rate.

But with a lower teaser rate, your lifetime cap is reduced also. If you have a lifetime cap of 6.00 percent, that cap is based on your starting rate. If one lender offers 4.00 percent and another offers 4.25 percent, all other things being equal, choose the lower rate because it also lowers your lifetime cap from 10.25 percent to 10.00 percent.

This might seem like a no-brainer, but it's not when you throw in lender junk fees and origination charges. Remember how to properly compare rates. A lower teaser rate might in fact not be your best deal if getting it costs you a lot more money.

CONFIDENTIAL: Your Margin Is Your Lender's Little Secret

ARMs can get lost in a sea of vocabulary. Start rates, LIBOR, annual caps, lifetime caps, fully indexed—it can get confusing. It's the margin that you need to concentrate on.

The margin determines how quickly your rate will rise. If one lender has a 2.00 percent margin and another lender has a 3.00 percent margin, you can see that the second lender will increase its rates 50 percent faster than the first.

You can have an identical start rate, but with a higher margin, your loan can move to its caps more quickly. In fact, it's not uncommon for lenders who offer lower start rates to offset that with a higher margin.

A common margin is 2.75 percent. You'll see this margin available in a variety of mortgage loans offered by lenders everywhere. Anything above that is nothing more than a lender's attempt to get more interest from you faster.

On the other hand, the margin might just be open for negotiation. Or at least you could "buy down" the margin, just as you might buy down a fixed-rate mortgage loan by paying a point. And although paying points to get a lower fixed rate may not always make sense, if you can buy your margin down, you need to explore this. Typical margin buy downs are much more generous than those reserved for fixed rates.

Getting a 1/2 percent margin reduction for a point is not uncommon. Here's an example.

Loan amount is	$300,000
Start rate	4%
Index: 1 year Treasury	4.50
Margin	2.75
Points	0
Fully indexed rate	7.25%

Now pay 1 point to buy your margin to 2.25:

Fully indexed rate	6.75%

On a $300,000 note, $^1/_2$ percent equals about $100. With an ARM, when you buy down the margin, you'll always enjoy that lower payment because of your caps and your margin. In this example, you paid $3,000 in points to reduce your monthly payment by $100. But you get this savings over and over again until and if you reach your lifetime cap.

When rates adjust, your adjustment will always be $100 less when you have a lower margin. That means for as long as you own the mortgage. Always ask for margin reductions. It may not be something that's printed on a lender's rate sheet, but it's worth inquiring.

CONFIDENTIAL: Your Lender May Try to Confuse You by Comparing ARM Loans with Different Indexes

Just as a lender that is not competitive on one particular loan type may try and steer you into one of its more competitive programs, a lender can also try to move you into another index.

This switch is common. If you're talking to a lender and it gives you a rate quote on one of its ARMs, it's likely that the loan officer won't tell you the index being used, even though that lender has ARM programs for almost every index imaginable.

If you've decided on an ARM and you call a lender and ask for its one-year ARM quote, you'll get the lender's most competitive ARM. Probably. But if you don't also ask for the index, you may be being quoted apples and oranges.

One index might be down for a few years or recent months, while another index might be trading up. You may not know the history of those indexes, and, quite honestly, even if you did, it would still be a toss-up. But if you simply get an ARM quote from one lender and then from another lender and then from another without knowing the index for any of those quotes, you're lost, and you're wasting your time.

ARMs can be confusing enough as they are without trying to cross-compare.

CONFIDENTIAL: Do Your Research and Choose an ARM Only When Rates Are at Relative Highs

Okay, here's the caveat: No one can accurately predict the future. But one can use the past as an indicator. The best web site I know for researching interest rates is at www.hsh.com. There are certainly other places, but this is the site I've always used, and it doesn't cost anything.

Interest rates moves in cycles; they go up, and they go down. But they don't move wildly. A one-year Treasury index won't go from 5.00 percent one day to 15.00 percent the next. Rather, they move in slower, incremental steps.

If rates are high compared to the recent past, you may want to consider getting an adjustable-rate mortgage. Because ARMs start out with lower teaser rates and have adjustment caps, your initial rate will be lower than those on current fixed-rate products.

And if you're lucky and you chose correctly, your adjustable rate will actually go down. Yes, you got the lower teaser rate, but because rates in general had started on a downward path, your mortgage payment actually went down—not up.

Yes, just as ARMs can go up, they can also go down. Quite a nice surprise, isn't it? Yes, those mean old lenders don't have it in for you every time, now do they? No, they can actually provide you with a nice annual present.

If during your research you see that interest rates are at highs not seen for four to five years, you should consider an ARM.

CONFIDENTIAL: Lenders Can't Predict the Future, and Neither Can You

If rates aren't that low, then check out their history and see whether rates are in fact on the upswing, staying the same, or potentially going down. This can be hard to do, but it can be done.

Back in the late 1990s, when low rates seemed as if they were setting records every day, many people chose ARMs. Instead of taking a fixed rate in the 7 percent range, which at the time seemed low, some consumers chose an ARM. What happened was that those consumers actually watched their mortgage rate drop and drop and drop.

Personally, I got a mortgage rate in the low 7 percent range in 1998. At the time, rates were at lows that had not been seen for years. So I locked this in with a 30-year rate. A couple of years later I refinanced into another fixed-rate loan, this time at 6.25 percent. Finally, in 2003, I refinanced one more time and secured a 5.00 percent 30-year fixed rate, which I'm still enjoying today.

At the same time, others were enjoying watching their mortgage payment actually fall automatically without the associated costs of refinancing. Rates seemed to be at relative lows in 1998, so most people took fixed rates. However, others took ARMs, and it was the people who had ARMs who finished in the money.

Was a 7.00 percent rate bad? Of course not. Historically, it was a great rate. Heck, I'm in the business, right? If I had thought that rates were going to continue to go down, I might have chosen an ARM.

A couple of years later, rates went down further still—to unheard-of fixed rates in the low 6.00 percent range. What did I do? I locked in that rate, of course. After all, rates couldn't get any lower than that, could they? If I had thought they were going to go down from 6.00 percent, I would have either waived and not refinanced or taken an ARM.

I assumed that rates couldn't get that much lower. They did. This time, I got another fixed rate. The point is that no one can tell what rates are going to do, so you have to make a prudent decision based upon historical evidence, advice from your loan officer, and anywhere else you can get a whiff of where rates are going.

CONFIDENTIAL: Some People Aren't Built for ARMs

I'm one of those people. I just don't have the stomach for it. I don't even visit Las Vegas. Okay, I do, but I don't gamble. Much. And to me, an ARM is a gamble. Even if I pick a rate at 7.00 percent, I can still tell you what my mortgage payment will be 10 years from now: 7.00 percent. I also have a very good friend who's been in the mortgage business for 20 years and has financed properties on his own for decades. His mortgage du jour? You guessed it: ARMs.

If having your mortgage payment fluctuate with the rate makes your stomach churn, then don't even consider an adjustable-rate mortgage, and for goodness' sake don't let a loan officer talk you into one. In my years of mortgage lending, there is a definite distinction between those who will take an ARM and those who want nothing to do with them.

Are you not sure if you want an ARM or not? Then perhaps you shouldn't take one. While ARMs have caps, they also have adjustments. And it's the fear of the unknown that can give you the creeps. Or not.

An ARM isn't something you should be talked into. If you call a lender and ask for its most recent fixed-rate quote and that lender isn't competitive at the moment, it will try to steer you toward an ARM. Don't let it. If an ARM isn't for you, it's not for you. You'll know it when you shop for mortgage rates.

But there's the opposite side of the mortgage coin: fixed rates. If ARMs aren't your cup of tea, then you need to look at a fixed rate.

CONFIDENTIAL: There Are Other Choices Besides a 15-Year and a 30-Year Fixed Rate

You just have to ask. There's a considerable difference in both payment and interest paid between a 30- and a 15-year fixed-rate loan.

A typical "spread" between a 30-year and a 15-year fixed rate is normally about ¹/₂ percent. If you can find a 30-year rate at 7.00 percent, then a similarly priced 15-year mortgage at most places will be in the 6.50 percent range. But when you figure your monthly payment, that's where the differences make you really stand up and take notice.

A 6.50 percent 15-year rate on $200,000 gives you a $1,735 monthly payment. A 30-year rate on the same day could be found at 7.00 percent, or a $1,325 monthly payment. That's quite a difference. People choose a shorter amortization period to save on interest paid to the lender. Each month, more of the payment goes toward the loan balance, with much less going to the lender. But the difference between monthly payments on a 15-year and a 30-year loan can be prohibitive. That's almost $400 per month. That's braces for your kid. Plus maybe part of a car payment.

There are other choices, but your lender won't advertise them. You have to ask. Mortgage loans can be offered to consumers in 10-, 15-, 20-, 25-, and 30-year terms. Lenders even offer mortgage loans amortized over 40 years. Even 50.

If you want to cut down on the interest paid on a longer-term mortgage, but you don't want the higher payments of a shorter-term one, choose something in between. A common choice is a 20-year loan.

A 20-year loan might be offered at 1/8 percent higher than the 15-year loan, but when you figure the monthly payment on $200,000 at 6.625 percent, the payment is only $1,507. That's in between the 30 and 15-year payments, and it can be a nice accommodation for those who are looking to both pay less interest and have a lower monthly payment.

If you ask your loan officer for a 20- or 25-year quote and she tells you the firm doesn't offer one, your loan officer is incorrect. Either ask her to check for you or find a loan officer with a little more experience.

CONFIDENTIAL: Hybrids Are a Nice Choice, but They're Still ARMs

Can't decide between a fixed-rate loan and an ARM? Does the 20-year rate thing not do much for you, and you still want a lower payment? Then a hybrid is probably your best choice.

A hybrid, while still an ARM, is so called because it acts like a fixed rate in the first few years, then morphs back into an annual ARM. Common hybrids are fixed for three and five years, but other hybrids can be found in the seven- to ten-year range.

Hybrids are listed as 3/1, 5/1, 7/1, and 10/1, indicating both how long the initial rate is fixed for and how often the loan adjusts after that period. A 3/1 ARM is fixed for three years, then turns into a one-year ARM. A 7/1 ARM is fixed for seven years, then adjusts to an annual ARM.

A 5/6? It's fixed for five years, then turns into a six-month ARM. A 14/4 hybrid? They don't make them, but if you figured it out, then you understand hybrids.

Hybrids are popular because they have a lower starting rate than fixed-rate mortgages but still give some added security in terms of knowing what the rate will be in the future.

Hybrids can also have varying indexes. You might find a lender offering a hybrid based upon a one-year Treasury, another lender with a LIBOR-based hybrid, and still other lenders offering all choices.

And as well as different indexes, there are also different margins. If you're looking at hybrid mortgages, then in reality the margin and index on which your loan is based will be insignificant. By the time the initial fixed period has ended, you've generally either refinanced or sold the property and moved on.

CONFIDENTIAL: Stay Away from Negative Amortization

With a name like that, who wouldn't stay away from negative amortization? Heck, I stay away from absolutely everything negative, and you do, too, right?

Negative amortization means that if you don't pay your loan's fully indexed rate, then the remaining payment will be added back to your loan balance. Your loan actually grows. It amortizes—negatively.

Think of it this way. You have a five-year car loan with an adjustable rate. You have a balance of $10,000. Your fully indexed payment is $300. But your car lender has been nice to you and has given you a choice of payments: the regular $300 payment, or a lower one of $200.

Who wouldn't choose the $200 payment? Well, you might not if you found out that the $100 difference would be added back to your loan.

After 10 months of making only the $200 payment and not the $300 one, another $1,000 has been added to your car loan.

After 10 months, and after making 10 payments, you not only haven't paid your car loan down, but you've actually added to it. Now, is that a good deal? No. It's not a good deal.

Negative-amortization loans, called "neg-am" loans, have been around for a long time. They fall out of favor because they're not good loans, so everyone forgets about them. Later, after everyone has forgotten about them, they rise from the mortgage grave and are given another name, and "voilà!": negative amortization. But it can kick people out of their homes.

If neg-am loans are so bad, then why do lenders even offer them? Negative amortization is a feature of some loans that have some fairly attractive features if borrowers understand when they can be used. Neg-am loans aren't bad by nature. They can have a place.

Neg-am is always associated with an adjustable-rate mortgage that offers a variety of loan repayment options. The neg-am feature gives mortgage owners a choice of what to pay each month, usually including the fully indexed rate. The neg-am kicks in when the borrowers decide not to pay the fully indexed rate, but instead to pay the lower "contract" rate. Some contract rates can be 1 percent. Or more, or less.

Having an option to pay less can be a benefit for someone who gets paid on an irregular basis, say someone who gets paid when a job gets completed, or maybe a business owner whose cash flow increases during holiday seasons, or maybe a commissioned salesperson who gets huge commissions during certain times of the year, but doesn't get much at other times.

The option can also be an advantage for landlords, who might like to pay the fully indexed rate when the rental unit is occupied, but might want to make only the lower payment if and when the unit is vacant.

Such payment choices can be a benefit to borrowers. They are able to pay more when they make a lot of money, then maybe pull back a tad when cash flow decreases. Understand that a neg-am loan, by itself, is not a bad thing if you know what you're doing.

CONFIDENTIAL: Don't Be Fooled by the Term *Potential* Neg-Am

Potential neg-am means the very same thing as a neg-am loan. The loan office might say, "Yes, potentially this can be a neg-am loan, but it's really not a neg-am loan."

That's what a neg-am loan is. If you don't make the fully indexed payment, the remainder of what you didn't pay gets added back to the original principal, causing your loan to grow. This again is negative amortization. There's nothing potential about it.

CONFIDENTIAL: Don't Be Fooled by "Payment-Option" Loans

Payment-option loan programs come in several varieties, but this is essentially another name for a neg-am loan.

Lenders give their loan programs different names for a variety of reasons. It's mostly done for marketing purposes, but in this case it's to hide the negative connotations that a neg-am loan has.

Perhaps one of the most common names for a neg-am loan is the "pick a pay" loan program. Sounds great, doesn't it? In fact, payment-option ARMs do have a potential neg-am feature, but they also throw in a fully amortized option.

This program will allow you to pay your contract rate, which can be below your fully indexed rate, causing you to negatively amortize; pay the fully indexed rate on an "interest only" option; pay the fully indexed rate on a fully amortized basis; or make a payment based upon a fixed-rate, fully amortized loan.

Yes, there are options. But quite frankly, why would you want them? There are people who simply want to have choices with their mortgage program, and the payment-option plan certainly offers them.

But if you want a fixed rate, this is not the program for you. These programs don't have the most competitive fixed rates in the market; the fixed rate is simply there as an option. Or if you want an ARM, take an ARM. But don't take one that has neg-am as a possibility.

CONFIDENTIAL: Interest-Only Loans Carry Additional Risk

Like never paying down your mortgage. An interest-only loan lets you pay simple interest on your mortgage, while also letting you pay down the principal at your leisure. The trap with interest-only mortgages is that if you don't get into the habit of paying additional principal every month, your original loan stays the same.

To calculate the payment on an interest-only loan, just take your loan amount and multiply it by the interest rate, then divide by 12.

If your rate is 5.00 percent and your loan is $400,000, then your interest-only payment is 5.00% × $400,000 = $20,000 divided by 12 = $1,667 per month. To compare that with a fully indexed 30-year fixed-rate loan at 5.00 percent, the monthly payment is $2,144.

That's quite a difference, and it also shows you how much goes toward your principal each month. You need to have the discipline to make principal payments, or else the interest-only loan can cause you problems.

CONFIDENTIAL: Zero-Money-Down Loans and Interest Only Don't Mix

If you don't pay your balance down and you use a zero-money-down loan, or perhaps even if you put 5 to 10 percent down, these loan programs can hurt.

Remember that it costs money to sell a home. Commissions, title insurance, legal fees—they all add up. If you put little or nothing down, you automatically have no equity. If you don't pay down your principal at all, you'll have to come to the closing table with money when you sell instead of taking money away.

Let's say you buy a home for $300,000 and put 5 percent down, and in three years you have to sell. Your loan balance at the beginning was $285,000. You also take out an interest-only loan and don't pay anything toward the principal during that same three-year period. Then you get transferred to another location and have to sell your home.

Closing costs on your sale might be $25,000. And unless your property has appreciated enough to cover those costs, your situation would look like this:

Sales price	$300,000
Loan payoff	$ 285,000
Closing costs	$ 25,000
Balance	($ 10,000)

To pull this deal off, you have to bring a check for $10,000 to closing. If you had put more money down to buy the property, say 10 to 20 percent, you would just skate by. Or if you put little or nothing down and had a fully amortized loan instead of paying interest only, you'd narrow your losses.

On a 6.00 percent 15-year fixed-rate loan with 5 percent down, loan amount $285,000, after three years, your loan balance would be about $246,000. With natural amortization, your equity position has grown, and now not only do you have enough to cover your payoff and your closing costs, but you actually take home $29,000.

With a zero-down loan under the same scenario, you've paid your original $300,000 loan to $249,000, still plenty of wiggle room. Even over such a short period as 36 months, a fully amortized fixed payment can pay down your loan.

But when you mix a no- or low-money-down loan with interest only, you're setting yourself up for a potential disaster.

CONFIDENTIAL: Prepayment Penalties Aren't Always a Bad Thing

A prepayment penalty is often associated with subprime loans. A prepayment penalty means that if the mortgage is paid off ahead of its normal term, say 30 years or 15 years or whatever the amortization period may be, then the borrower must pay the lender a predetermined amount of money.

Prepayment penalties are a form of mortgage interest. It's interest that you would have paid had you not paid off the loan or refinanced out of it. Lenders who offer prepayment penalties do so because they recognize two things:

There's a higher risk in the loan because of the buyer's credit.

There's a higher risk that the loan will be refinanced out of as soon as the borrower is able to do so.

When a lender makes a loan with a prepayment penalty, the lender is able to offer a lower interest rate than it otherwise might if the borrower didn't agree to the prepayment penalty clause.

If a borrower has damaged credit and the lender wants to make a mortgage loan, the lender will offset part of that risk with a penalty.

And because subprime loans are higher in rate than conventional ones, borrowers attempt to repair their credit as soon as possible in order to get out of the higher-rate loan and refinance into a lower-rate, conventional product.

CONFIDENTIAL: Prepayment Penalties Can Be "Hard" or "Soft"

Note that different states may have different definitions of what constitutes a prepayment penalty and in some instances may even regulate when and if prepayment penalty clauses can be inserted into mortgage loans.

A penalty will apply if the original note is paid off by selling the home and paying off the mortgage, by refinancing the loan and replacing it with another one, and finally by the borrower's making extra payments or principal paydowns. Any of these three events can trigger a penalty.

A hard penalty applies if any of these three events happens. If the borrower so much as pays $10 extra toward the note, the penalty can kick in. Some lenders, however, choose to implement a "soft" penalty.

A soft penalty will allow for principal paydowns and does not apply if the home is sold to someone else. It applies only during a refinance, and it applies for a shorter term. A soft penalty would typically apply only during the first two or three years of the original loan and would be counted toward only 80 percent of the outstanding balance.

That 80 percent rule means that you can make extra payments during any 12-month period as long as those payments do not exceed 20 percent of the outstanding principal balance. If you have a $100,000 mortgage, you can pay extra without any penalty whatsoever as long as you do not exceed $20,000 in extra payments during any consecutive 12-month period.

Soft penalties are rather lenient.

A hard penalty will normally be six months' worth of interest. If you have a $350,000 loan and your rate is 8.50 percent, you can expect to pay nearly $15,000 in interest in the form of a penalty to the lender if you refinance or otherwise pay off your loan. Check with your accountant, but as prepayment penalties are mortgage interest, to help soften the blow, that $15,000 could be tax-deductible.

A soft penalty on that same $350,000 at 8.50 percent would, first, apply to only 80 percent of $350,000, or $280,000. Now calculate the 8.50 percent on $280,000, and the penalty is $11,900, representing six months of outstanding interest.

Soft penalties are designed to discourage refinancing. They do not hamper a homeowner if the homeowner decides to sell, but are applied only if the homeowner pays off the loan directly or refinances it.

CONFIDENTIAL: Some Prepayment Penalties Can Be Bought Out

Upon loan approval, some lenders who impose prepayment penalties may offer to get rid of the prepayment penalty portion of the loan altogether at a price.

Most usually, however, this option applies only to soft penalties, not to hard ones. If there is a prepayment penalty on an offered loan program, the borrower may be able to buy out the penalty or reduce its term.

Normal buyouts are 1 discount point for each year bought out. If there is a three-year penalty on a loan, the consumer can opt to reduce that term to two years by paying 1 point at closing or to one year by paying 2 points, and so on.

And just as with other rate/point combinations, the interest rate can be adjusted upward to offset the penalty as well. When given this option of paying points or raising the rate, it often makes sense to raise the rate.

If you buy out a prepayment penalty, you're fairly certain that you're going to retire the note more quickly. That said, paying anything up front isn't a good idea, but bearing a higher monthly payment for a shorter period of time might make sense.

Let's say you have a two-year hybrid with a two-year prepayment penalty, and your loan amount is $200,000. If you paid 2 points to get rid of your penalty, you would pay $4,000.

On the other hand, if you increased your interest rate by $1/2$ percent, to 8.00 percent from 7.50 percent, your monthly payment would go up by only about $70. Two years' worth of $70 is just $1,680. That's much less than the points you would have paid.

There can be different types of buyout pricing with different lenders, but if you have the option of increasing your rate rather than paying anything up front, you'll almost always come out ahead.

CONFIDENTIAL: Don't Be Talked Into Any Particular Type of Loan

If you feel as if you're being rushed into something, take a few steps back. Mortgage lending and its terminology can be confusing and intimidating. Mortgage loan officers place loans every day, so they can sometimes appear a little callous about the situation. After all, when they close your loan, they move onto the next one, while you're still making payments every month.

Choosing the best loan program for you doesn't have to be a mind bender. But when one loan officer is competing for your business with another loan officer, you're often suddenly presented with a baffling array of mortgage choices.

If and when you get confused, and you feel as if you're being pushed around, remember who's in control here—it's you.

Mortgages come in two flavors, fixed and adjustable, with a hybrid thrown in between. Keep your individual goals in mind, consider how long you're going to be owning the home or otherwise keeping the mortgage, and make the determination from there.

Are you a short termer? Do you see yourself owning the home for just a few years before selling it and buying "up"? Is this not your first home? Is this a home you'll be keeping for a long, long time? Do you want to cut down on the amount of interest you pay?

These questions, when asked of either a fixed-rate or an adjustable-rate loan, will help you determine which loan program best suits your needs. Remember who the boss is.

C H A P T E R   8

Refinancing

A refinance is taking one loan and replacing it with another. A refinance can be helpful if you want to lower your interest rate, you want to pull some additional equity out of your home, you want to make some improvements, or you want to combine different loans into one. Most often, though, a refinance takes place when borrowers want to reduce their monthly payments.

CONFIDENTIAL: Don't Wait Until Rates Are 2.00 Percent Below Your Current Rate Before You Refinance

This "2.00 percent rule" has been around forever, it seems. It simply doesn't make sense, and, quite frankly, it never did. The idea may generally work, since most consumers don't have a mortgage calculator handy or know how to calculate a mortgage payment by hand. Nor do they have an idea of the closing costs associated with mortgage loans.

Usually, though, a consumer has a handle on what his current rate and monthly payment are. If you have a mortgage at 9.00 percent and rates are 7.00 percent, then it would make sense to refinance. But the real way to determine whether or not a refinance is worth your while is to consider both the new monthly payment and the associated closing costs that will accompany the new loan.

Let's look at an example.

Current mortgage balance	$225,000
Current mortgage rate, term	6.25%, 30-year fixed
Closing costs	$3,800
Current monthly payment	$1,477
Estimated years of future ownership	10

Suppose mortgage interest rates have dropped to 5.50 percent, or 0.75 percent lower than your current rate. Refinancing into an identical 30-year mortgage at 5.50 percent yields a new payment of $1,277. That's a $200 difference.

Now divide that monthly payment into the closing cost figure of $3,800 to get how many months it will take to "recover" the closing fee, and the result is 19 months. Not bad. All in all, if you can recover your closing costs as a result of the new lower payment in a couple of years or so, then it might make sense to refinance your current mortgage.

In this example, you paid the $3,800 out of pocket rather than adding it into the current loan. When refinancing, it's common and permissible to roll closing costs into your mortgage balance. If we added the $3,800 to $225,000, the final loan amount would be $228,800. The new monthly payment at 5.50 percent would be $1,299. That's still not a bad deal.

CONFIDENTIAL: Don't Pay Points or Origination Fees When Refinancing

Just as taking points and origination charges into consideration for a purchase loan, you must look even more closely at points or origination charges when you refinance. If 1 point gets you a $1/4$ percent interest-rate reduction, the new lower payment rarely pays for the point that you paid.

Using that same $225,000 loan balance and on the same current terms, you could find a 30-year rate of 5.25 percent, but you would pay 1 point for it, or $2,250. The new monthly payment would drop only to $1,242, or $35 lower than $1,277.

And you paid the point for that privilege, or $2,250 for $35 per month. Divide those numbers and you arrive at 64.3 months to recover the money you paid in points.

When you're rate shopping and you're being quoted a rate with a point on it, get the rate quote that's just a bit higher. You should expect a $1/4$ percent increase in rate when you remove the point from the equation. If you get a loan officer who won't budge on the point or quotes you something much higher in rate for the 1-point trade-off, find another lender.

CONFIDENTIAL: Don't Pay Any Closing Costs When Refinancing

Instead, look at increasing your interest rate by enough to cover your closing costs. This is the "no points, no fee" refinance that you see advertised. You in fact do pay it; it's just in the form of a higher rate.

How do you determine a fair exchange between a higher rate and no closing costs? First, take your closing cost figure, then divide that amount by your loan amount. By dividing $3,800 by $225,000, you get 0.017, or 1.7 points.

If you increase your rate by $1/4$ percent for each point, this calculation would get you a 30-year fixed rate of about 5.875 to 6.00 percent. At 6.00 percent, the new monthly payment would be $1,348. That's higher than $1,277 by $71.

But you paid no closing costs; the lender paid them for you in exchange for a higher rate. You dropped your monthly payment by $129 per month—for free. There is no cost recovery period. Could you have gotten a lower payment? Sure, but you would have paid $3,800 up front to do so.

CONFIDENTIAL: You Might Be Able to Reduce Your Note Rate Without Refinancing at All

A little-known secret in mortgage lending is called a *note modification*. The name makes what you're accomplishing fairly clear: You are modifying your current note.

As rates move down from what you currently have, you'll begin to get solicitations from your lender about refinancing. "Refinance now while rates are low!" and so on. And not only solicitations from your current lender. Your e-mail box and your post office box will be crammed with refinancing offers.

Every one of them will be offering about the same rates, terms, and payments. But they can't modify your note. Only your original and current lender can. And don't expect your lender to contact you to see if you want to modify your note. Why would it? It's happy just the way things are, thank you very much.

It's up to you to contact your lender and ask for a note modification. If you call the customer service number and say "modification," they may think you're trying to explain a refinance to them, when in fact you're suggesting anything but.

No, a note modification is approved, priced, and granted through your lender's secondary department, not through regular retail channels.

A note can be modified only if your current lender was also the original lender. If your note has been sold to another lender, then you may not have a modification option. There are in fact a few modifiable notes in the market today where the note can be modified no matter who currently owns the mortgage, but for some reason those particular notes never took off with lenders, so there aren't many of them out there.

In fact, if you ask your prospective lender if the mortgage you're applying for has a "modification feature," it's likely that your loan officer won't know what you're talking about. If this happens to you, have your loan officer call the lender and ask it directly on your behalf. Most notes do not have a modification feature. So this approach can work only if your original lender hasn't sold your loan.

You will either contact your original loan officer or contact the secondary department. There's a telephone number on your mortgage statement that you can call. Specifically ask the secondary department if your note allows you to modify. If you can, you can expect:

A marginal modification fee, maybe $300 or so

An interest rate that's slightly higher than what you could get in the open market (but lower than what you've been paying)

There's no reason for a secondary department to offer the absolute best rate available. It won't do that; instead, it will calculate a "make sense" number for you—higher than what's on the street, but still low enough for you to do it rather than refinancing your loan entirely and sending it to a brand new lender.

If you can drop your rate from 7.00 percent to 6.00 percent and it costs you hardly anything and doesn't involve inflating your rate to cover third-party fees, then a note modification is the way to go. Hands down.

CONFIDENTIAL: Cash-Out Refinancings Can Cost You More Than You Think

A common practice of loan officers is to suggest that you pay off consumer loans with a lower, tax-deductible mortgage rate. Refinance your current loan and pay off your credit cards, your car loan, your student loans—heck, whatever you want!

This number trick usually works. Rates on automobile loans and credit cards are always higher than mortgage rates, and the new monthly payments are always lower. But be careful; remember that loan officers don't get paid until they close a loan, so they're always thinking of ways to get you to apply for a new mortgage with them.

All that is okay, just evaluate a refinance with cash pulled out in other ways as well.

Let's look at our $225,000 refinance at 6.00 percent, with a new payment of $1,348. Now we want to pull cash out to:

Pay off an auto loan $10,000   8.00% $202 monthly payment
Pay off credit cards $30,000   12.00% $300 minimum monthly payment

When the auto loan and the credit card balances are added into the mortgage, the new monthly payment at 6.00 percent is $1,588. That's higher than the current mortgage payment of $1,477, but still lower than the current payment of $1,477 plus the $202 car payment and the $300 credit card bill, or $1,979. The numbers work, at least on paper.

The difference is only in the monthly payment. Yes, you've gotten rid of your automobile payment, but what was on a 5-year note is now stretched out over 30 years. A 5-year auto loan carries interest charges of $2,165. Stretching that same $10,000 over 30 years at 6.00 percent results in interest charges of $11,583, which is almost another car, or at least part of another one.

Yeah, I know, I know. No one carries a note out for 30 years, and the auto loan isn't tax-deductible, but it's still a big difference.

Credit card bills? Okay, that's a bigger difference, and it's revolving debt, not installment debt like a car. But the fact is that most people don't pay off the credit card and leave it at a zero balance; instead, they begin charging on it again.

After a few years, you've bought a new car, you're still making the mortgage payment on the old one, and your credit card balances are where they were when you first used equity in your home to pay off both balances.

And you get another call from your loan officer suggesting that you might want to pay off your credit cards and other debt while refinancing your current mortgage.

Are cash-out refinancing deals good things or bad things? They're usually good things, but don't get a cash-out refinance just to pay something off. Instead, consider one if you were going to refinance your note anyway because of the lower rates available. Don't do it because some loan officer showed you how much lower your payments would be if you consolidated your bills.

CONFIDENTIAL: Higher Loan-to-Value Cash Outs Carry Higher Rates

Your loan-to-value, or LTV, number can affect your cash-out interest rate. When a cash-out refinance approaches 70 percent of the appraised value of your home, you can expect to pay more for that extra cash. Lenders can charge another $1/4$ percent if you pull equity out of your home in the form of a cash-out refinance and your loan balance is more than 70 percent of the value of your home. They can charge still more if the loan exceeds 75 percent of the value of the home, and a lender flat out won't do a refinance if the loan exceeds 80 percent of the home's value.

The difference is usually about 1 discount point or $1/4$ percent in rate when you exceed 70 percent of the value of the home. If the value of your home is $300,000, you can take cash out along with your mortgage refinance up to 70 percent of $300,000, or $210,000.

If you had a mortgage balance of $180,000 and borrowed $210,000, you would cash out about $30,000, less closing costs. But if you borrowed 75 percent of $300,000, or $225,000, you would cash out $45,000. And since you exceeded the 70 percent LTV guideline, you would also have to pay another 1 point, or $2,250.

At 75 percent LTV, you got $15,000 more in cash in your pocket. But you had to give an additional $2,250 to do so. It's not worth it. If at all possible, stay below the 70 percent cash-out limit.

CONFIDENTIAL: Explore an Equity Loan in Lieu of a Cash-Out Refinance

Your loan officer won't make anything on an equity loan, but she will on a refinance, so you may not hear many pitches for an equity loan from a loan officer. But it's something to consider if you don't really want to refinance right now.

An equity loan is a loan made against the free equity you have in your home. If the value of your home is $300,000 and your current loan balance is $200,000, then you have $100,000 in equity.

Equity loans are typically "second" mortgages; they're in second position, behind your current first mortgage. Second mortgages are also always cheap when compared to first notes.

Equity loans carry few closing costs, if any. They can be one lump-sum payment that you pay off over the years, or you can get a line of credit that you can draw against when you need it.

In fact, most banks offer equity lines to their customers and don't charge them anything at all. No title insurance or attorney fees or appraisal charges—they're free. That is, an equity loan is free if the borrower draws against it at some point during the year. Otherwise there might be a nominal $200 "inactivity" fee. (Can you believe it!)

Equity loans in the form of one lump sum can have either fixed or adjustable rates; equity lines have adjustable rates. The better your credit, the higher the LTV that your line can have. If you have excellent credit, you can expect an equity line of up to 100 percent of the value of the property. With less than excellent or just plain good credit, maybe the line will go up to 90 or 95 percent.

CONFIDENTIAL: When Buying, an Equity Loan Can Replace Your Down Payment at Closing

This process involves an equity loan, but it is a bit odd because the equity loan in this case is actually a refinance, or at least a loan that is taken out after the purchase has been recorded.

For instance, you're buying a new home for $400,000, you put 20 percent, or $80,000, down, and at the very same time you apply for an equity line of $80,000. This means that even though you put down your

$80,000, you also immediately have a credit line in the exact amount of your down payment available to you. Yes, you have to have the $80,000 in the first place, but you have that same $80,000 immediately available to you right after you close.

In effect, you've just gotten yourself a zero-down loan program with no mortgage insurance. Quite a deal, really. It's a perfect strategy to get a good first mortgage rate, temporarily use your liquid funds to close the deal, then have access to a credit line almost immediately upon closing.

These lines will be found only through banks that are also offering your first mortgage, and you can't find them through many mortgage bankers or mortgage brokers unless one of them has arranged financing with a retail bank channel that offers such a combination.

CONFIDENTIAL: When Rates Are Low, It's Better to Secure a Fixed Rate

Refinancing isn't always done just to lower the rate or pull out equity in the form of cash. If you buy a house when rates are peaking, chances are you'll choose an adjustable-rate loan to keep the payments down, and that's most likely a good call.

But when rates begin to drift downward and you have the opportunity to lock in a fixed rate, if you intend to keep the property for several more years, it makes sense to refinance out of an adjustable-rate mortgage and into a fixed-rate one.

When rates begin to drop, the temptation is to follow those rates as low as they can go. This means getting an adjustable-rate mortgage. Resist the urge and secure those low fixed rates.

CONFIDENTIAL: There Are Ways to Save on Closing Costs When Refinancing That Weren't Available to You When You Bought

The first person to ask is the lender or broker that you worked with previously. Call that person first and say, "I'm thinking of refinancing my mortgage. Since you already have my original loan application, I want you to waive your fees."

Most likely, you'll get most, if not all, of the junk fees waived. But you have to ask.

Title insurance is probably the biggest savings. And title insurance can be expensive; in fact, it is one of the most expensive items on the settlement statement. Title insurance is an insurance policy that insures the lender, the sellers, and the buyers that the transfer of property ownership is safe and secure, without any defects such as previous claims on the property, forgery, or fraud.

For example, suppose one party sells a home to another, then one day there's a knock on the door and it's some guy who says, "Hi, I actually received one-tenth of this house from my grandfather 20 years ago, and I own part of it. It was sold to you illegally, so now please get out of the house," or some such frightening event.

Title insurance is typically issued upon transfer of ownership, and when someone refinances, ownership is not transferred; it's the same owner. Still, a new title insurance policy must be in force with each new loan, refinance or no. There are discounts available for such short-term policies, but often you have to ask.

Title insurance requirements vary from state to state, and so do the discounts available. What is eligible for a discount in Texas will be completely different from the discounts available in California.

The most common discount on title insurance is called a *reissue*, whereby the same owners take out a new policy that covers the time from their original purchase (or last refinance) up until the new refinance loan.

A reissue rate is available, but depending upon where you live, you won't necessarily get it automatically. In fact, in some states where a reissue rate is available, the new policy must be replaced by one from the same insurance company, not a new one.

Still other areas simply verify that ownership has not changed hands since the original purchase, and any title insurance company can provide the lower-priced policy.

If your title insurance company is holding your closing, acting as your escrow agent, or otherwise providing more than one product or service, ask for a discount on those services.

A title insurance company may have an escrow department that will hold your closing as well as issuing title coverage. Or the attorney who is handling your transaction may also supply title insurance or other services that might come at a discount.

Another common savings is with a survey. In many states, lenders require that a survey be completed before a new loan is placed. But what if you already have a survey? Lenders will accept an old survey as long as there were no changes to the property since the original survey was done. Even then, if the survey is older than 10 years, the lender may not take it at all, and a new one will be required.

A survey will show your property lines, where your house sits on the property, fences, sidewalks, decks, and, perhaps most importantly, easements. An easement is a legal right of a third party, usually a utility or city government, to access your property whenever it sees fit.

A common example is an easement that is granted to a cable television company. If you have one of those cable TV boxes in your backyard, the cable company has a right to access your property whenever it needs to fix something.

Or your survey will show a line going across your backyard, indicating that a utility line is buried beneath the surface.

A survey will also show a swimming pool in your yard, or a storage shed, or a fence. One reason that a lender wants a new survey is that there is no other way to determine if any changes have been made since your old survey was performed.

Did the electricity company build a new utility line that runs through your backyard? Did you add a fence? A rock wall? Yes, you may have had a survey performed four or five years ago, but it won't resemble the new one if you've made permanent changes to your property. The only ways around this are to have a new survey done or to sign an affidavit stating, "I have not made any changes to the property since the last survey."

It may also be possible to eliminate the need for an appraisal when refinancing. You'll need to ask for this option when you make your application, but there are loan programs that do not require a complete appraisal, but are dependent instead upon the AUS issuing the approval. Freddie Mac loans, for example, have an option for either a reduced appraisal or an exemption. In this case, you could save $300 or more.

CONFIDENTIAL: When You Pull Cash Out, the Lender Will Ask You What You're Going to Do with the Money—Be Careful with Your Answer

Don't lie, just be careful. College education? Vacation? Home improvements? Quitting your job and starting a new business?

I've seen this happen before: The borrower was pulling money out of a home, and in the section where the 1003 asks "Purpose of Loan Proceeds," the borrower has said, "Starting a new business."

This new business wasn't something that the buyer was going to quit her old job for; she was simply starting another business for her spouse, a child, or a family member.

But answering "starting a new business" will put an underwriter on notice that you may be quitting your job—the job that the underwriter is using to qualify you. "Oh, really," says the underwriter. "Can you tell me a little more about this new job?" You're stuck. You'll have more explaining to do, so why even mess with the details?

This question on the 1003 is an old one, and one day it will be phased out because its utility simply isn't there. The fact is that proceeds from a cash-out refinance should be used for whatever you're going to invest those funds into.

Are you going to invest in a home improvement? Invest in a vacation? Invest in the stock market? Invest in a business?

By simply answering the question with the word *invest*, you're both answering the 1003 and providing a clear answer. There's no need to muddy up anything. Just answer the questions and move on.

CONFIDENTIAL: You Still Have to Qualify for a Refinance, Just as You Did for the Purchase

Let's say you've got a 30-year fixed-rate mortgage at 8.00 percent, and rates have dropped to 5.00 percent. Your payments are going from $2,200 to $1,600! You can't wait!

But you've had some problems since you first bought your house. Your credit has been damaged because of a job situation, and it's getting harder and harder to pay the bills. So what better way to help ease the cash flow pain each month than with a lower mortgage payment, right?

Hold on. Just because your payment would drop doesn't mean that you're going to get that new loan. It's possible that even though you would have a lower monthly payment, you still may not qualify if there are some credit issues that have arisen since you first bought the house.

You'll need to qualify all over again. I know, I know. It may not make sense at first glance. If you can pay your mortgage now, then why couldn't you pay it more easily when you've reduced your payment by a couple of hundred bucks?

The fact is that every new loan is a brand new loan, refinance or not. And the loan has to be underwritten in the same way as the loan you took out when you bought the house. Your credit, your debt ratios, and other risk elements will be reviewed all over again.

CONFIDENTIAL: You Can't Add Someone to a Refinance to Help You Qualify

While adding someone to a mortgage when buying a home can sometimes help from an income-to-debt ratio standpoint, adding someone to a refinance to help you qualify isn't allowed.

One important factor with your original mortgage is that you agree not to alter the ownership of the property without the lender's knowing about it. For instance, this means that you can't give the house away to someone else. If you do so without permission, the lender can call in the note immediately. This is called *acceleration*, because the mortgage term is accelerated from 30 years from now to "tomorrow."

When would someone give away a house? It can happen often when the original owner wants out from under the obligation; he can deed the home to a family member, or perhaps "sell" the property to someone else under a rent-to-own scenario or some other unofficial property transfer.

And just as you can't alter the ownership without the lender's permission, you also can't alter the ownership to help you qualify if you're having trouble qualifying for a refinance.

Unfortunately, this happens when there are issues beyond the homeowner's control, almost always when bad things like divorce, a death in the family, or loss of a job happen. The only way out of such a scenario is to qualify by yourself. Adding someone else does no good, and it is against your original agreement.

CONFIDENTIAL: If You Have an FHA or VA Loan and Want to Refinance and Your Credit Has Been Damaged, You're in Luck: You Can "Streamline"

VA and FHA offer a type of refinance called a "streamline." If you have a VA or an FHA mortgage and your credit has suffered since the original purchase, you're fortunate. Both agencies can allow a refinance into a new, lower-rate mortgage as long as the new mortgage does not exceed the current balance (no cash out, for example) and your monthly payment goes down. This is easy enough to prove, easy to close, and simple to qualify for, as long as your mortgage payment was never more than 30 days past the due date.

CONFIDENTIAL: When You Refinance, You're Not Skipping Payments

This is a common advertisement: "Refinance with us . . . skip your next payment!" or "Refinance now—no house payments for two months!"

This is not true, but since most consumers aren't aware of how they pay mortgage interest to their lender, it might seem like it. Since mortgage interest is paid in arrears, it's easy to understand how consumers can be misled.

Mortgage payments are made "backward," whereas rent payments are made "forward." When renters pay rent on the first of every month, they're paying for the month they've not yet lived in the property. They're paying rent ahead of time.

When homeowners make a mortgage payment on the first of the month, they're paying for the month they've already lived in the property. Mortgage interest accrues daily, based upon the mortgage's rate and term, and is then due on the first of the following month.

During a refinance, the prospective mortgage lender will contact the current lender for a "payoff." The payoff is the outstanding loan amount still due, plus the amount of interest that will accrue during the month in which the loan is paid off.

For example, if a refinance loan will fund on the 20th of the month, the new lender will send a written request for a mortgage payoff. The payoff will show the current principal balance, the rate, and the daily interest that will accrue and be due at closing.

Using a 30-year fixed rate of 6.50 percent on an original loan balance of $250,000, the per diem, or daily interest accrual on that note, is about

$52 per day. The lender will multiply $52 by the number of days to the 20th of the month, when the loan is scheduled to fund.

The new loan is not the unpaid balance, but the unpaid balance plus accrued interest. In this example, it would be the $250,000 balance plus 20 days of accrued interest at $52 per day, or $1,040.

The $1,040 is added to the $250,000 to make a loan payoff to the old lender of $251,040. Because interest is paid in arrears, the interest for the month has yet to be paid, and is most often rolled into the new loan.

One doesn't "skip" a payment; instead, the interest yet to be paid for the month in which the loan was made was rolled into the new loan, just like any other closing cost. You borrowed next month's house payment.

So how does one "skip" two payments? By not making the current month's mortgage payment, which rolls in the previous month's accrued interest, and by rolling in the following month's mortgage payment.

Nothing is skipped; it's just added to the loan balance. Lenders that advertise "skipping" when you refinance with them are misleading you.

CONFIDENTIAL: The Best Time to Close a Refinance Is as Close to the First of the Month as Possible

This also means that you are closing your mortgage as soon as you can when rates are low. Since interest accrues, it accrues at the older, higher rate. Each day you delay, you're paying more.

You may have heard that the best time to close a purchase mortgage is at the end of the month, primarily to save on accrued interest charges, but when you refinance a note and you like the rates available for your refinance, then by all means don't tarry. I've seen people with high interest rates wait and wait and wait for rates to go down "just a tad more" when what they're really doing is offsetting any gains they would have gotten had they refinanced into available lower rates.

The main difference between a purchase loan and a refinance loan lies in when the rate must be locked in. In a purchase transaction, one must find a lender, find a rate, and lock that rate in a week or two before the scheduled closing. If your closing is taking place within 30 days, you have about 20 days to look for a lender and a rate.

In a refinance, you can shop till the cows come home. There is no specified date on which you're supposed to close. Heck, you can quit the process any time you want to. Often, though, that waiting game yields negative results.

Let's say you have an 8.00 percent rate and a $300,000 loan, and rates are now at 5.00 percent. By refinancing at the lower rate, you save $590 per month, or about $20 per day. The 5.00 percent rate may be readily available, but, being the economic guru that you are, you're convinced that the unemployment numbers coming out next month are going to be worse than expected, meaning that there are lower rates ahead. After all, you might gain another $1/4$ percent, right?

What's the difference between 5.00 percent and 4.75 percent? About $1.50 per day.

So instead of cashing in all your chips and your $590 per month savings, you wait another month for the next unemployment report. You could have saved $590, but you're trying to squeeze everything you possibly can out of the deal. You "lost" the $590 savings you could have had by trying to get another $1.50 per day.

In trying to save another $45 per month, you're already behind because you didn't lock in the 5.00 percent and begin saving as soon as you could. And guess what else? The unemployment number you were banking on was actually better than expected, so rates went up—you guessed wrong.

By waiting until the end of the month, or until next month, you may be losing money. Lock in sooner rather than later.

C H A P T E R 9

Buying and Building New

When you buy a newly built home, there are some special considerations that you need to be aware of. This is different from most existing home sales. Developments are financed and sold differently from existing homes, and builders make their money in a tad different fashion.

CONFIDENTIAL: Using a Realtor Will Save You Money

If you're not using a Realtor, you should be. Realtors will save you time and money. And the neat thing about it is that they're free. When you use a Realtor to find a home to buy, it's not you who pays the commission—it's the seller or the seller's Realtor that pays it.

A typical commission to sell real estate might be 6 percent of the sales price. On a $150,000 home, that comes to $9,000. If a home shopper drives by a home that is listed for sale and makes an offer that is accepted, the seller of the home will pay the listing agent the $9,000 in real estate commissions.

If a Realtor finds the home for his clients, and an offer is made and is accepted, the listing agent will typically split that $9,000 right down the middle with the Realtor who brought the buyers to the table. You don't pay; the seller pays.

What a deal, right? Where else can you get such valuable service and pay nothing for it?

There are some parts of the country where buyers pay Realtors for certain buyer's services, and in still other areas, builders don't pay Realtors who find buyers anything, but all in all, a buyer's Realtor is free. Get one. Because you'll need one.

There are certain performance clauses in new construction, things that say "on such and such a date, this much of the home will be completed" or "at this point, this home will be X percent done," and so on.

Realtors will also help you properly review the deal and prepare an offer that makes sense for you and protects your interests.

If Realtors in your area get commissions from builders, you really are better off getting one.

CONFIDENTIAL: If There Are Any Special Business Relationships Between the Builder and Other Businesses, You Need to Know About Them Before You Go Any Further

Builders, just like people in any other business, can have special relationships with other companies. Often the businesses they have these relationships with include mortgage companies. Some of the bigger national builders own their own mortgage operations, while others work with local companies. Whatever the case, it is a legal requirement that any special business relationships that have been established must be disclosed to you.

Why is this important to you? If a builder is referring you to third parties, don't you want to know if he's just doing it out of the kindness of his heart or if he's getting part of the action?

If a title insurance policy costs you $1,000 and the builder encourages you to use a particular title company, wouldn't it be helpful to you to know that the builder gets 10 percent of whatever the title agency sells?

Often these arrangements are called controlled business arrangements, or CBAs. Or they may be called affiliated business arrangements, or ABAs. Whatever the arrangement and whatever it's called, there's a law saying that you must know about any special deals and sign a piece of paper acknowledging that fact.

If you're encouraged to use a particular title company, a particular attorney, a particular mortgage company, or anyone else, you're supposed to know how "special" those special relationships really are.

CONFIDENTIAL: Your Contract Could Spell Disaster

Perhaps the most critical element of buying new is how your contract is worded. You can get yourself into some very hot water if you're not careful. The builder wants you to have an enjoyable experience, but the builder is also doing it to make money. You buy a house you like from the builder; he gets money from you.

The contract spells out what is expected of you and what the builder is expected to do. Perhaps the most important part of the contract concerns your mortgage and where you can get it from.

If a builder owns a mortgage company or has an ABA with a mortgage operation, it's likely that you will be required to complete a loan application with that mortgage operation.

Your contract won't require you to take a loan from that mortgage firm, but you will most often be required to apply nonetheless.

This is the tricky part—be careful about how this section is worded. If all the contract says is, "As part of this agreement, you, the buyer, will apply for a mortgage from my mortgage company within five days," you're fine. You're not required to use the builder's mortgage company; you merely must apply.

But it can get confusing fast. The contract can also say, "As part of this agreement, you, the buyer, will apply for a mortgage from my mortgage company within five days. If we get you an approved loan and you do not use our mortgage company for your home loan, you will lose your deposit of $50,000."

I recently received an e-mail from a buyer in the Washington, DC, area who was in a real pickle. He was buying a new home, but he couldn't sell his old one in time. He needed the money from the old home to put down on his new one. But the old house wasn't moving—there was absolutely no traffic.

It came down to 10 days before closing, and the builder wanted the mortgage information. After all, as part of the contract, the buyer was required to apply at the builder's mortgage company, and if the builder's mortgage company offered him a loan and he didn't take it, he would lose all $65,000 of his deposit money.

The buyer didn't use the builder's mortgage company, but instead found one on his own. But because he hadn't sold his own home, his debt ratios were too high for him to be approved by anyone. In fact, his debt ratios were nearly 100. He had to be qualified using both house payments, and when added together they almost equaled his monthly gross income.

That meant that after taxes, he was automatically "upside down" with his payments. He simply couldn't afford the new home, so he withdrew his offer.

"Not so fast," said the builder. "Our contract says that if we offered you a loan, then you would take it or else lose your $65,000." The builder had in fact offered the buyer a home loan, one that used no income documentation whatsoever and had a sky-high interest rate.

Put both house payments together, and his ratios hit 125.

"But I can't afford those payments!" said the buyer.

"Sorry, the contract says nothing about that," said the builder. "Move in, or lose $65,000."

Had the buyer used a Realtor to help negotiate his contracts, this probably would not have happened because the Realtor would have changed the wording. The contract should have been changed to read, "If the builder's mortgage company offers you a mortgage with an interest rate of 7.00 percent or below and you have sold your old home and you don't take the loan, you'll lose your $65,000."

Now it's a little fairer. Now the builder is convinced that this is a serious buyer, and the buyer knows that this is serious business. Now she needs to go get financing to close the deal, and she's obligated to use the builder's company as long as its rates are below 7.00 percent and she's sold her home.

CONFIDENTIAL: Separate the Cost of the Upgrades from the Cost of the House

An incentive to use or not use a builder's mortgage company can take many, certainly enticing forms. One of the more common enticements is upgrades.

"Use our lender and we'll throw in $10,000 worth of upgrades!" says your builder. Does that sound like a lot to you? It does to me. Why would a builder give away $10,000 in upgrades to have the mortgage company make $3,000 in origination fees? It doesn't make sense.

Maybe the upgrades aren't worth $10,000 after all. Or maybe the builder will make it up on the next house sold to some poor soul who isn't nearly as fortunate as you. If you don't know the true cost of upgrades prior to considering such an offer, you're truly at a disadvantage.

Instead, very early in the home buying process, before you make any mortgage application whatsoever, find out what upgrades you want and don't want, and what they might cost. If you're asking about the cost of upgrades at the very same time the builder is telling you that it will give you $10,000 in upgrades if you take the loan from the builder's mortgage company, it's a little late for that.

When negotiating the price of a home, leave the upgrades out of the equation. Instead, ask about the price of each individual set of upgrades as if you were choosing them from a list.

"We really have only $10,000 to spend on upgrades, so we really need some choices." This might help you pare down your list and perhaps get a better handle on how much those upgrades really cost.

Are your upgrades something you can quantify? Can you take the builder's quote, then go to a major home center and have it quote the very same thing? You may find out that the upgrades you're getting are worth less than the price you're being quoted. In all fairness, they can also be worth much more. But do your own research first.

Another common incentive the builder will offer is to pay for certain closing costs should you decide to use its lender. A common cost might be for title insurance, some discount points, or origination fees.

This approach by the builder is something you can get an easier handle on. While upgrades may be difficult to put a dollar sign on, you can compare closing costs more easily by reviewing your GFE.

Either way, you need to determine if in fact the builder's mortgage company is competitive. Is the builder giving you a $3,000 discount if you use its mortgage company, but the mortgage company charges about $3,000 more than everyone else? Where do you think the builder is getting the funds to give to you? Could it be from higher rates?

Make sure you compare the quotes from builder-owned mortgage companies with the quotes from all the other mortgage companies you've talked to. Don't sign any agreement until you've evaluated all the options and assigned values to the various incentives the builder is offering you.

CONFIDENTIAL: The Builder's Lender Is Probably a Mortgage Broker

That's not a bad thing by any means; it's just that this is a common arrangement. If in fact the builder's mortgage company is a mortgage broker, then that broker could have access to a number of lenders and to loan programs that your bank may not be able to offer.

It also means that the builder's mortgage company gets its mortgage pricing from the exact same places that other mortgage brokers in your area get them, and this is an easy way to determine if you're getting a competitive quote or not.

If one broker is offering you 6.00 percent and no points, but the builder is offering you either 6.25 percent and no points or 6.00 percent at 1 point, but also paying 1 point toward your closing costs, you can see where these various builder incentives sometimes originate.

If you're being quoted higher, then simply ask the broker, "Why are you higher than the other mortgage brokers I've gotten quotes from?" and then show her the GFEs and rate quotes you've received from her competitors.

CONFIDENTIAL: Developers Don't Get Paid Until the Very End of a Project

Why is that important? Because at the end of a project, when the builder starts making a profit, it's possible that better deals can be struck.

When a builder builds out a development, he borrows some money, lots of it, to use to draw plans, buy hammers and nails, and pay for construction crews. Let's say a builder borrows $10 million to build 50 homes and will make a profit of $2 million.

As each home is sold, the money goes to pay for the overhead, the hammers and nails, the salaries, and, most of all, interest to the lender who doled out the $10 million. As each day passes, the builder is accruing interest owed to the construction lender. If there are delays in construction for any reason, from lack of skilled labor to simply bad weather, the builder has to pay more money.

So he wants to sell his homes as fast as he can to pay off the $10 million loan. It's not until the note is paid off that the builder gets to make his real profits. That's why at the last stage of a development, the builder might be more inclined to cut some deals, to get his profit into his bank account sooner rather than later.

You can feel more confident in bargaining with your builder's mortgage company when you're buying one of the few houses that have yet to have sold and closed.

CONFIDENTIAL: Your Builder Doesn't Care About the Origination Fee

That's why these various "use my lender and I'll give you $10,000 in upgrades" tend not to make sense. Yes, the builder may have a financial interest in the mortgage company you use, but the real reason it may want you to use its lender is not for the origination fee but for the control it has.

Because interest accrues daily, along with higher overhead and employee costs, builders can be relatively stern when it comes to a closing date. If the builder puts a house under contract, it has effectively taken that home off the market. The builder will set a closing date of "end of this month" and will expect a check. The sooner that check comes in, the better to avoid interest charges.

But what if suddenly the deal falls through? Then the builder has to scramble to find another buyer and find one fast. When a buyer uses the builder's mortgage company, all the builder has to do is make a phone call or stick her head in some loan officer's door and say, "Hey, how's the Smith deal going?" to get an updated response.

No one likes surprises, especially if they cost thousands of dollars. Builders like their customers to use their mortgage company to help them control their inventory of homes, and ultimately their profit margin. You can now see why they really, really want you to use their mortgage operation.

CONFIDENTIAL: Construction Loans to Build a Custom Home Have a Whole New Set of Concerns

But what if you aren't buying in a new development? What if you want to build your own home where you want to build it?

This brings up different considerations altogether. When you buy in a development, there are typically several builders that have different sets of plans for you to choose from. You look at the plans, negotiate the price, get preapproved, put down your deposit, and wait for the home to be built.

When you are financing the construction of your very own home, you need to acquire the land if you don't already own it, get house plans and specifications from an architect and builder, get quotes to build the house, get construction lending, then finally get your mortgage.

Although a construction loan covers the cost to build your home, you will soon need a permanent mortgage to take its place. And just as with a purchase mortgage, you need some sort of down payment. When you improve a lot by building a home on it, that land is now part of your equity—your down payment.

Construction loans are short-term in nature; they last only as long as it takes to build your home. At the end of construction, your bank wants its money back, plus interest.

When you decide to build, you can have an architect design your home, or you can find a home design that you like from any of various home plan companies. You take your plans to different builders, who will soon deliver to you their bid to build.

After you get your bids and have decided on a builder, you take that bid to your construction lender, which will help pay everyone when they need to be paid. If your plan says it's going to cost $450,000 to build your home, that figure is arrived at by adding up:

Labor

Materials

Permits

Now that the $450,000 is tallied, you choose your construction lender.

CONFIDENTIAL: Although Construction Loans Can Be Found at Many Lenders, It Pays to Work with a Construction Loan Officer

I've closed over 1,000 mortgage loans, but I've closed only a handful of construction loans. Fortunately for me, I had staff that took over the administration of my construction loans for me.

With a mortgage, you get underwritten and approved, then you show up with your down payment and closing cost money. Not so with construction loans.

A construction lender won't look at your $450,000 construction quote, call the builder, and hand her a check for $450,000. That would be too much of a risk.

Instead, construction funds are doled out in phases as the work progresses. When the site is cleared and the slab is poured, the builder will usually present an invoice and receipts showing how much she has done on the job so far. The bank will then send out either an appraiser or a bank officer to physically visit the job site and say, "Yep, the site has been cleared and the slab has been poured."

The bank then issues a check to the builder to cover the costs of either the work just completed or the next phase of construction. A few weeks later, another invoice and receipts appears, claiming, "I've just completed the framing, truss, and plumbing."

Again, there's a visit by the bank, and again, the bank officer confirms that the work is or is not complete. The bank then issues another check. This process is repeated until the home is completed.

If you don't use a loan officer who is experienced with this kind of "fund control," then you can expect some problems. Most loan officers close a deal, collect their check, and go home. Construction projects aren't completed for several months. You can't afford to have your loan officer not show up for an inspection or otherwise slow down the construction. You need someone who can help you navigate.

CONFIDENTIAL: The Slower the Construction Period on Your Project, the More Money You Have to Pay

When you get a construction loan, it's like a line of credit. You don't actually begin paying interest on the loan until you start to pay off the builder. If your builder submits an invoice showing that $50,000 worth of work has been done and/or the bank approves the next phase, that is the point when you begin paying interest, and you pay it only on the $50,000 you have drawn.

If there are delays in your construction project or if your bank or mortgage company loan officer can't get to the job site to confirm progress, you're paying for those delays. One of the many reasons to choose a particular builder, in addition to the quality of work, is the builder's ability to build and close on schedule.

If you have withdrawn $100,000 so far and suddenly everything comes to a standstill, then it doesn't really matter why construction has stopped—you're still paying interest on the money that was withdrawn to pay the builder.

At the end of construction, your construction loan will be replaced by a regular mortgage. Your new mortgage company will contact your construction lender for a final payoff figure and use those numbers as the basis for your loan amount.

Unless you have arranged for zero percent down financing, you'll need to have some type of down payment.

CONFIDENTIAL: Owning Your Own Lot Is Automatic Equity in Your New Home

If you own a lot that's worth $20,000 vacant and you build on it, suddenly the $20,000 lot plus the home on top of it is worth more than if they were valued independently. If your construction loan payoff is $450,000 and your lot value is worth $20,000, then suddenly you'll see your total value exceed the sum of these figures, automatically. A lot with a house on it is worth a lot more than a home without a lot and the equity you have in the land.

You now need to consider getting mortgage insurance or getting subordinate financing, since your loan amount is 90 percent of the value of the home. But because you own the lot and the lot provides additional value, you've already invested 10 percent in the deal.

CONFIDENTIAL: Construction Loans Are Easy to Compare

Just look at the rate. Most construction lenders know their competitors like the back of their hand, so you won't find a wild array of closing cost and rate combinations. You'll probably get nearly identical quotes in terms of closing costs.

But just as when you compare mortgage quotes, you need to separate the lender fees from the nonlender fees. The nonlender fees will be the same regardless of which construction lender you choose, but mostly will include title insurance, surveys, county and government charges, and other assessment fees.

The rate is typically the key, and most likely it will be the same from one lender to another. Most construction loans come from retail banks that have a construction lending division, staffed with loan officers, inspectors, and those who control the construction funds.

All things being equal, your construction loan quotes should be very, very similar. Most construction quotes are at prime, prime plus 1, or some variation thereof. That being said, the first place you should look is the bank where you keep your checking account.

Getting a construction loan from the same place that you have other depository accounts can often get you additional perks, such as free checking, a free safe deposit box, and other free "bank stuff."

CONFIDENTIAL: When You Are Constructing Your Home, Your Permanent Mortgage May Not Be Locked In

You have two loans in progress; one is for construction, and one is for the permanent mortgage. You know ahead of time what your construction loan rate will be, but it's not likely that you know what your permanent loan rate will be. It's too far out to lock in.

As your home gets closer to being completed, you should be considering getting your permanent financing lined up. You do this the very same way you shop for other mortgages, as described in Chapter 5.

You compare rates and fees, and you make sure your rate is locked in far enough in advance to cover your closing date.

However, you're a captive of what the market is doing, so you have to keep your fingers crossed that no upward rate swings happen while your home is being built. When you get about 60 days away from your scheduled close date, you should seriously consider locking in your rate with your chosen mortgage lender.

You're also held captive by your builder. If he's been on time so far with everything else during your construction, then your scheduled completion date should be on schedule as well. But if your builder continuously has delays, whether or not they're his fault—be careful.

If your closing date is extended, this will affect your lock period. If your lock expires because of your builder, don't expect any sympathy from the mortgage company.

CONFIDENTIAL: You Can Guarantee Your Interest Rate on Both the Construction Loan and the Permanent Mortgage, While Cutting Down Closing Costs, with a One-Time Close Loan

This is a relatively new development over the past few years. You can't find loans of this type at mortgage brokers or most mortgage bankers. Instead, you find them at mortgage bankers that have both a construction department and a secondary department, and there aren't that many of them compared to the total number of available mortgage loan sources in the marketplace.

One-time close loans are just that; there is one close. You don't go to one closing for your construction and another for your permanent mortgage; you just have one closing.

A common marketing ploy with a one-time close loan is that you don't have to pay two sets of closing costs. While that is true, it's also true that having two separate closings doesn't automatically mean that your closing costs double.

You'll save some closing fees on a one-time close loan, but you'll most likely save about 20 to –30 percent when compared to two closings. That's significant, but it's not half off.

One-time close loans also guarantee what your interest rate will be at the end of the construction period. There is no guessing, and there is no shopping for a permanent mortgage; it's built right into your loan program.

At the end of construction, your loan goes automatically to its predetermined rate. And there's an added benefit: Not having to go to another closing is worth a lot in terms of simply making arrangements to show up.

CONFIDENTIAL: If Rates Have Gone Down During Construction and They're Much Lower Than Your Predetermined Permanent Rate, Ask Your Lender for a Reset

Lenders recognize that markets can move. And if rates go down during your construction to, say, 6.00 percent and you're locked in at 7.50 percent, then guess what you're going to do? That's right, find a mortgage somewhere else during construction.

Just as a refinance is used to pay off another mortgage, a refinance can also be used to pay off a construction loan. Often your lender will give you a list of its current rate offerings about 30 days before your scheduled completion date and let you have a choice. Don't expect to get its absolutely best rate, but you can expect to be 1/8 percent or so out from that. That's not a bad deal at all, considering the additional closing costs you would incur if you decided to refinance elsewhere.

Conversely, if rates go up during your construction period, you're locked in. These loans are really the best of both worlds: getting competitive construction quotes, closing once, and having your permanent mortgage rate guaranteed.

If you're going to build your own home, you'll be hard-pressed to find a better alternative than a one-time close loan.

CONFIDENTIAL: Commitment Fees Are Not Uncommon with Construction Loans

These fees typically represent 1 percent of the loan amount. If you sign loan papers and are asked to pay a 1 percent origination fee, it's really a commitment fee. That fee is nonrefundable.

Some loan officers charge a 1 percent fee up front simply to keep you from shopping other lenders while your home is being built. Some loan officers will take 1 percent from you at your initial closing, then "refund" that 1 percent origination fee when you close on your permanent loan.

This is usually nothing more than holding some of your money as an insurance policy should you decide to change lenders at the very end. If you paid a $3,000 commitment fee that is refundable, but you change lenders at the end of construction, then you've lost that $3,000 commitment fee. Your loan officer splits that money with his company.

CONFIDENTIAL: Your Construction Loan Lender May Require a Contingency Fund

Most often, this is 10 percent of your construction loan. It is there to cushion the blow should change orders occur during construction. If you have a $300,000 construction quote, your contingency fund would be $30,000.

If your contingency fund isn't used, you don't pay any interest on it, but it's there just in case. If you don't want a contingency fund, ask your loan officer if it's a requirement of the loan or simply a suggestion.

Another loan increase might be in the form of an "interest reserve," which is an amount that the bank loans you so that you can make your rental or house payments while your home is being built. You can take the reserve and add it to your construction loan or make the payments on your own as they arise.

Either way, you need to know if there is a contingency or interest reserve fund being added to your loan amount that you didn't request. Neither is necessarily a bad thing by any means, but it should be a conscious choice on your part one way or the other.

Payment Tables

Payments per Thousand Dollars Financed

Find the interest rate, move across to the Term column, and multiply that number by the number of thousand dollars financed.

Example: 6.50 percent, 30-year term on $150,000

$6.32 × 150 (thousands) = $948.00 principal and interest payment

Rate	40 years	30 years	25 years
2.500	$ 3.30	$ 3.95	$ 4.49
2.625	$ 3.37	$ 4.02	$ 4.55
2.750	$ 3.44	$ 4.08	$ 4.61
2.875	$ 3.51	$ 4.15	$ 4.68
3.000	$ 3.58	$ 4.22	$ 4.74
3.125	$ 3.65	$ 4.28	$ 4.81
3.250	$ 3.73	$ 4.35	$ 4.87
3.375	$ 3.80	$ 4.42	$ 4.94
3.500	$ 3.87	$ 4.49	$ 5.01
3.625	$ 3.95	$ 4.56	$ 5.07
3.750	$ 4.03	$ 4.63	$ 5.14
3.875	$ 4.10	$ 4.70	$ 5.21
4.000	$ 4.18	$ 4.77	$ 5.28

Rate	40 years	30 years	25 years
4.125	$ 4.26	$ 4.85	$ 5.35
4.250	$ 4.34	$ 4.92	$ 5.42
4.375	$ 4.42	$ 4.99	$ 5.49
4.500	$ 4.50	$ 5.07	$ 5.56
4.625	$ 4.58	$ 5.14	$ 5.63
4.750	$ 4.66	$ 5.22	$ 5.70
4.875	$ 4.74	$ 5.29	$ 5.77
5.000	$ 4.82	$ 5.37	$ 5.85
5.125	$ 4.91	$ 5.44	$ 5.92
5.250	$ 4.99	$ 5.52	$ 5.99
5.375	$ 5.07	$ 5.60	$ 6.07
5.500	$ 5.16	$ 5.68	$ 6.14
5.625	$ 5.24	$ 5.76	$ 6.22
5.750	$ 5.33	$ 5.84	$ 6.29
5.875	$ 5.42	$ 5.92	$ 6.37
6.000	$ 5.50	$ 6.00	$ 6.44
6.125	$ 5.59	$ 6.08	$ 6.52
6.250	$ 5.68	$ 6.16	$ 6.60
6.375	$ 5.77	$ 6.24	$ 6.67
6.500	$ 5.85	$ 6.32	$ 6.75
6.625	$ 5.94	$ 6.40	$ 6.83
6.750	$ 6.03	$ 6.49	$ 6.91
6.875	$ 6.12	$ 6.57	$ 6.99
7.000	$ 6.21	$ 6.65	$ 7.07
7.125	$ 6.31	$ 6.74	$ 7.15
7.250	$ 6.40	$ 6.82	$ 7.23
7.375	$ 6.49	$ 6.91	$ 7.31
7.500	$ 6.58	$ 6.99	$ 7.39
7.625	$ 6.67	$ 7.08	$ 7.47
7.750	$ 6.77	$ 7.16	$ 7.55
7.875	$ 6.86	$ 7.25	$ 7.64
8.000	$ 6.95	$ 7.34	$ 7.72
8.125	$ 7.05	$ 7.42	$ 7.80
8.250	$ 7.14	$ 7.51	$ 7.88
8.375	$ 7.24	$ 7.60	$ 7.97
8.500	$ 7.33	$ 7.69	$ 8.05
8.625	$ 7.43	$ 7.78	$ 8.14
8.750	$ 7.52	$ 7.87	$ 8.22
8.875	$ 7.62	$ 7.96	$ 8.31
9.000	$ 7.71	$ 8.05	$ 8.39
9.125	$ 7.81	$ 8.14	$ 8.48
9.250	$ 7.91	$ 8.23	$ 8.56

Rate	40 years	30 years	25 years
9.375	$ 8.00	$ 8.32	$ 8.65
9.500	$ 8.10	$ 8.41	$ 8.74
9.625	$ 8.20	$ 8.50	$ 8.82
9.750	$ 8.30	$ 8.59	$ 8.91
9.875	$ 8.39	$ 8.68	$ 9.00
10.000	$ 8.49	$ 8.78	$ 9.09
10.125	$ 8.59	$ 8.87	$ 9.18
10.250	$ 8.69	$ 8.96	$ 9.26
10.375	$ 8.79	$ 9.05	$ 9.35
10.500	$ 8.89	$ 9.15	$ 9.44
10.625	$ 8.98	$ 9.24	$ 9.53
10.750	$ 9.08	$ 9.33	$ 9.62
10.875	$ 9.18	$ 9.43	$ 9.71
11.000	$ 9.28	$ 9.52	$ 9.80
11.125	$ 9.38	$ 9.62	$ 9.89
11.250	$ 9.48	$ 9.71	$ 9.98
11.375	$ 9.58	$ 9.81	$10.07
11.500	$ 9.68	$ 9.90	$10.16
11.625	$ 9.78	$10.00	$10.26
11.750	$ 9.88	$10.09	$10.35
11.875	$ 9.98	$10.19	$10.44
12.000	$10.08	$10.29	$10.53
12.125	$10.19	$10.38	$10.62
12.250	$10.29	$10.48	$10.72
12.375	$10.39	$10.58	$10.81
12.500	$10.49	$10.67	$10.90
12.625	$10.59	$10.77	$11.00
12.750	$10.69	$10.87	$11.09
12.875	$10.79	$10.96	$11.18
13.000	$10.90	$11.06	$11.28
13.125	$11.00	$11.16	$11.37
13.250	$11.10	$11.26	$11.47
13.375	$11.20	$11.36	$11.56
13.500	$11.30	$11.45	$11.66
13.625	$11.40	$11.55	$11.75
13.750	$11.51	$11.65	$11.85
13.875	$11.61	$11.75	$11.94
14.000	$11.71	$11.85	$12.04
14.125	$11.81	$11.95	$12.13
14.250	$11.92	$12.05	$12.23
14.375	$12.02	$12.15	$12.33
14.500	$12.12	$12.25	$12.42

Rate	40 years	30 years	25 years
14.625	$12.22	$12.35	$12.52
14.750	$12.33	$12.44	$12.61
14.875	$12.43	$12.54	$12.71
15.000	$12.53	$12.64	$12.81
15.125	$12.64	$12.74	$12.91
15.250	$12.74	$12.84	$13.00
15.375	$12.84	$12.94	$13.10
15.500	$12.94	$13.05	$13.20
15.625	$13.05	$13.15	$13.30
15.750	$13.15	$13.25	$13.39
15.875	$13.25	$13.35	$13.49
16.000	$13.36	$13.45	$13.59
16.125	$13.46	$13.55	$13.69
16.250	$13.56	$13.65	$13.79
16.375	$13.67	$13.75	$13.88
16.500	$13.77	$13.85	$13.98
16.625	$13.87	$13.95	$14.08
16.750	$13.98	$14.05	$14.18
16.875	$14.08	$14.16	$14.28
17.000	$14.18	$14.26	$14.38
17.125	$14.29	$14.36	$14.48
17.250	$14.39	$14.46	$14.58
17.375	$14.49	$14.56	$14.68
17.500	$14.60	$14.66	$14.78
17.625	$14.70	$14.77	$14.87
17.750	$14.80	$14.87	$14.97
17.875	$14.91	$14.97	$15.07
18.000	$15.01	$15.07	$15.17

Rate	20 years	15 years	10 years
2.500	$ 5.30	$ 6.67	$ 9.43
2.625	$ 5.36	$ 6.73	$ 9.48
2.750	$ 5.42	$ 6.79	$ 9.54
2.875	$ 5.48	$ 6.85	$ 9.60
3.000	$ 5.55	$ 6.91	$ 9.66
3.125	$ 5.61	$ 6.97	$ 9.71
3.250	$ 5.67	$ 7.03	$ 9.77
3.375	$ 5.74	$ 7.09	$ 9.83
3.500	$ 5.80	$ 7.15	$ 9.89
3.625	$ 5.86	$ 7.21	$ 9.95
3.750	$ 5.93	$ 7.27	$10.01
3.875	$ 5.99	$ 7.33	$10.07

Rate	20 years	15 years	10 years
4.000	$ 6.06	$ 7.40	$10.12
4.125	$ 6.13	$ 7.46	$10.18
4.250	$ 6.19	$ 7.52	$10.24
4.375	$ 6.26	$ 7.59	$10.30
4.500	$ 6.33	$ 7.65	$10.36
4.625	$ 6.39	$ 7.71	$10.42
4.750	$ 6.46	$ 7.78	$10.48
4.875	$ 6.53	$ 7.84	$10.55
5.000	$ 6.60	$ 7.91	$10.61
5.125	$ 6.67	$ 7.97	$10.67
5.250	$ 6.74	$ 8.04	$10.73
5.375	$ 6.81	$ 8.10	$10.79
5.500	$ 6.88	$ 8.17	$10.85
5.625	$ 6.95	$ 8.24	$10.91
5.750	$ 7.02	$ 8.30	$10.98
5.875	$ 7.09	$ 8.37	$11.04
6.000	$ 7.16	$ 8.44	$11.10
6.125	$ 7.24	$ 8.51	$11.16
6.250	$ 7.31	$ 8.57	$11.23
6.375	$ 7.38	$ 8.64	$11.29
6.500	$ 7.46	$ 8.71	$11.35
6.625	$ 7.53	$ 8.78	$11.42
6.750	$ 7.60	$ 8.85	$11.48
6.875	$ 7.68	$ 8.92	$11.55
7.000	$ 7.75	$ 8.99	$11.61
7.125	$ 7.83	$ 9.06	$11.68
7.250	$ 7.90	$ 9.13	$11.74
7.375	$ 7.98	$ 9.20	$11.81
7.500	$ 8.06	$ 9.27	$11.87
7.625	$ 8.13	$ 9.34	$11.94
7.750	$ 8.21	$ 9.41	$12.00
7.875	$ 8.29	$ 9.48	$12.07
8.000	$ 8.36	$ 9.56	$12.13
8.125	$ 8.44	$ 9.63	$12.20
8.250	$ 8.52	$ 9.70	$12.27
8.375	$ 8.60	$ 9.77	$12.33
8.500	$ 8.68	$ 9.85	$12.40
8.625	$ 8.76	$ 9.92	$12.47
8.750	$ 8.84	$ 9.99	$12.53
8.875	$ 8.92	$10.07	$12.60
9.000	$ 9.00	$10.14	$12.67
9.125	$ 9.08	$10.22	$12.74

Rate	20 years	15 years	10 years
9.250	$ 9.16	$10.29	$12.80
9.375	$ 9.24	$10.37	$12.87
9.500	$ 9.32	$10.44	$12.94
9.625	$ 9.40	$10.52	$13.01
9.750	$ 9.49	$10.59	$13.08
9.875	$ 9.57	$10.67	$13.15
10.000	$ 9.65	$10.75	$13.22
10.125	$ 9.73	$10.82	$13.28
10.250	$ 9.82	$10.90	$13.35
10.375	$ 9.90	$10.98	$13.42
10.500	$ 9.98	$11.05	$13.49
10.625	$10.07	$11.13	$13.56
10.750	$10.15	$11.21	$13.63
10.875	$10.24	$11.29	$13.70
11.000	$10.32	$11.37	$13.78
11.125	$10.41	$11.44	$13.85
11.250	$10.49	$11.52	$13.92
11.375	$10.58	$11.60	$13.99
11.500	$10.66	$11.68	$14.06
11.625	$10.75	$11.76	$14.13
11.750	$10.84	$11.84	$14.20
11.875	$10.92	$11.92	$14.27
12.000	$11.01	$12.00	$14.35
12.125	$11.10	$12.08	$14.42
12.250	$11.19	$12.16	$14.49
12.375	$11.27	$12.24	$14.56
12.500	$11.36	$12.33	$14.64
12.625	$11.45	$12.41	$14.71
12.750	$11.54	$12.49	$14.78
12.875	$11.63	$12.57	$14.86
13.000	$11.72	$12.65	$14.93
13.125	$11.80	$12.73	$15.00
13.250	$11.89	$12.82	$15.08
13.375	$11.98	$12.90	$15.15
13.500	$12.07	$12.98	$15.23
13.625	$12.16	$13.07	$15.30
13.750	$12.25	$13.15	$15.38
13.875	$12.34	$13.23	$15.45
14.000	$12.44	$13.32	$15.53
14.125	$12.53	$13.40	$15.60
14.250	$12.62	$13.49	$15.68
14.375	$12.71	$13.57	$15.75

Rate	20 years	15 years	10 years
14.500	$12.80	$13.66	$15.83
14.625	$12.89	$13.74	$15.90
14.750	$12.98	$13.83	$15.98
14.875	$13.08	$13.91	$16.06
15.000	$13.17	$14.00	$16.13
15.125	$13.26	$14.08	$16.21
15.250	$13.35	$14.17	$16.29
15.375	$13.45	$14.25	$16.36
15.500	$13.54	$14.34	$16.44
15.625	$13.63	$14.43	$16.52
15.750	$13.73	$14.51	$16.60
15.875	$13.82	$14.60	$16.67
16.000	$13.91	$14.69	$16.75
16.125	$14.01	$14.77	$16.83
16.250	$14.10	$14.86	$16.91
16.375	$14.19	$14.95	$16.99
16.500	$14.29	$15.04	$17.06
16.625	$14.38	$15.13	$17.14
16.750	$14.48	$15.21	$17.22
16.875	$14.57	$15.30	$17.30
17.000	$14.67	$15.39	$17.38
17.125	$14.76	$15.48	$17.46
17.250	$14.86	$15.57	$17.54
17.375	$14.95	$15.66	$17.62
17.500	$15.05	$15.75	$17.70
17.625	$15.15	$15.84	$17.78
17.750	$15.24	$15.92	$17.86
17.875	$15.34	$16.01	$17.94
18.000	$15.43	$16.10	$18.02

Glossary

Abstract of title. A document used in certain parts of the country when determining if there are any previous claims on the property in question. The abstract is a written record of the historical ownership of the property and helps to determine whether the property can in fact be transferred from one party to another without any previous claims.

Acceleration. Paying off a loan early, usually at the request or demand of the lender. This is usually associated with an acceleration clause within a loan document that states what must happen when a loan must be paid immediately, but it most usually applies when payments are late or missed or there has been a transfer of the property without the lender's permission.

Adjustable-rate mortgage. A loan program where the interest rate may change throughout the life of the loan. The rate is adjusted based on terms that have been agreed upon by the lender and the borrower, but typically it will change only once or twice a year.

Amortization. The length of time it takes for a loan to be fully paid off, with repayment through equal payments made at regular intervals. Sometimes called a "fully amortized loan." Amortization terms vary, but generally accepted terms run in 5-year increments from 10 to 40 years.

Appraisal: A report that helps to determine the market value of a property. This report can be prepared in various ways as required by a lender, from simply driving by the property in a car to a full-blown inspection complete with photographs of the real estate with full-color pictures. Appraisals compare similar homes in the area to substantiate the value of the property in question.

APR. Annual percentage rate. The APR is the cost of money borrowed, expressed as an annual rate. It is a useful consumer tool for comparing different lenders, but unfortunately it often is not used correctly. The APR is useful only when the same exact loan type is being compared from one lender to another. It doesn't work as well when comparing different types of mortgage programs with different down payments, terms, and so on.

Assumable mortgage. A mortgage that lets buyers take over the terms of the loan along with the house being sold. Assumable loans may be fully qualifying or nonqualifying. With nonqualifying assumable loans, buyers can take over the loan without having to be qualified or otherwise evaluated by the original lender. With qualifying assumable loans, while buyers may assume the terms of the existing note, they must qualify all over again as if they were applying for a brand new loan.

Automated valuation model. An electronic method of evaluating a property's appraised value by scanning public records for recent home sales and other data in the subject property's neighborhood. This is not yet widely accepted as a replacement for full-blown appraisals, but many people expect to see AVMs replacing traditional appraisals altogether.

Balloon mortgage. A type of mortgage where the remaining balance must be paid in full at the end of a preset term. A 5-year balloon mortgage might be amortized over a 30-year period but have the remaining balance be due, in full, at the end of 5 years.

Banker. A lender who uses its own funds to lend money. Historically, these funds would have come from the savings accounts of other bank customers. But with the evolution of mortgage banking, that's the old way of doing business. Even though bankers use their own money, it may come from other sources, such as lines of credit, or from selling loans to other institutions.

Basis point. $1/100$ of 1 percent. 25 basis points is $1/4$ discount point. 100 basis points is 1 discount point.

Bridge loan. A short-term loan that is primarily used to pull equity out of one property for a down payment on another. This loan is paid off when the original property is sold. Since these are short-term loans, sometimes just for a few weeks, only retail banks generally offer them. Usually the borrower doesn't make any monthly payments and pays off the loan when the property is sold.

Brokers. Mortgage companies that set up a home loan between a banker and a borrower, similar to the way an independent insurance agent operates. Brokers don't have money to lend directly, but have experience in finding various loan programs that can suit the borrower. Brokers don't work for the borrower, but instead provide mortgage loan choices from other mortgage lenders.

Bundling. The act of putting together several real estate or mortgage services in one package. Instead of paying for an appraisal here and an inspection there, some or all of the buyer's services are packaged together. Usually this allows the service provider to offer discounts on all services, although when the services are bundled, it's hard to look at all of them to see whether you're getting a good deal or not.

Buydown. Paying more money to get a lower interest rate. This is called a permanent buydown, and it is used in conjunction with discount points—the more points, the lower the rate. A temporary buydown is a fixed-rate mortgage that starts at a reduced rate for the first period, and then gradually increases to its final note rate. A temporary buydown for two years is called a 2-1 buydown. A buydown for three years is called a 3-2-1 buydown.

Cash out. Taking equity out of a home in the form of cash during a refinance. Instead of just reducing your interest rate during a refinance and financing your closing costs, you finance even more, putting the money in your pocket.

Closing costs. The various fees involved when buying a home or obtaining a mortgage. The fees can come directly from the lender or may come from others in the transactions that provide services that are required to issue a good loan.

Collateral. Property owned by the borrower that is pledged to the lender in case the loan goes bad. A lender makes a mortgage with the house as collateral.

Comparable sales. The part of an appraisal report that lists recent transfers of similar properties in the immediate area of the house being bought. Also called "comps."

Conforming loan. A Fannie Mae or Freddie Mac loan that is equal to or less than the maximum allowable loan limits established by these organizations. These limits are changed annually.

Conventional loan. A mortgage using guidelines established by Fannie Mae or Freddie Mac and issued and guaranteed by a lender.

Credit report. A report showing a consumer's payment history along with the consumer's property addresses and any public records.

Debt consolidation. Paying off all or part of one's consumer debt with equity from a home. This can be part of a refinanced mortgage or a separate equity loan.

Debt ratio. Gross monthly payments divided by gross monthly income, expressed as a percentage. There are typically two debt ratios to be considered: The housing ratio (sometimes called the front ratio) is the total monthly house payment plus any monthly tax, insurance, PMI, or homeowners' association dues divided by gross monthly income, and the total debt ratio (also called the back ratio) is the total housing payment plus other monthly consumer installment or revolving debt, also expressed as a percentage. Loan debt ratio guidelines are usually denoted as 32/38, with 32 being the front ratio and 38 being the back ratio. Ratio guidelines can vary from loan to loan and lender to lender.

Deed. A written document evidencing each transfer of ownership in a property.

Deed of trust. A written document giving an interest in the home being bought to a third party, usually the lender, as security.

Delinquent. Being behind on a mortgage payment. Delinquencies typically are recognized as 30 + days delinquent, 60 + days delinquent, and 90 + days delinquent.

Discount points. Percentages of a loan amount; 1 point equals 1 percent of a loan balance. Borrowers pay discount points to reduce the interest rate on a mortgage, typically lowering the interest rate by $^1/_4$ percent for each discount point paid. It is a form of prepaid interest to a lender. Discount points are supposed to lower the rate. Also called "points."

Document stamp: Evidence of how much tax was paid—usually with a literal ink stamp—upon transfer of ownership of property. Called a "doc stamp" in certain states. Doc stamp tax rates can vary based upon locale. Some states don't have doc stamps; others do.

Down payment. The amount of money initially given by the borrower to close a mortgage; it equals the sales price less financing. It's the very first bit of equity you'll have in the home.

Easement. A right of way previously established by a third party. Easement types can vary, but they typically involve the right of a public utility to cross your land—for example, to access an electrical line.

Equity. The difference between the appraised value of a home and any outstanding loans recorded against the property.

Escrow. A term with two meanings, depending upon where you live. On the West Coast, there are escrow agents whose job it is to oversee the closing of a home loan. In other parts of the country, an escrow is a financial account set up by a lender to collect monthly installments for annual tax bills and/or hazard insurance policy renewals.

Escrow agent. On the West Coast, the person or company that handles the home closing, ensuring that documents are assigned correctly and property transfer has taken place legitimately.

Fannie Mae. Federal National Mortgage Association. Originally established in 1938 by the U.S. government to buy FHA mortgages and provide liquidity in the mortgage marketplace. Similar in function to Freddie Mac. In 1968, its charter was changed, and it now purchases conventional mortgages as well as government ones.

Fed. The Federal Reserve Board. The Fed, among other things, sets overnight lending rates for banking institutions. It doesn't set mortgage rates.

Fee income. Closing costs received by a lender or broker that are neither interest nor discount points. Fee income can be in the form of loan processing charges, underwriting fees, and the like.

FHA. Federal Housing Agency. Formed in 1934 and now a division of the Department of Housing and Urban Development (HUD), it provides loan guarantees to lenders who make loans following FHA guidelines.

Final inspection. The last inspection of a property, showing that a new home that is being built is 100 percent complete or that a home improvement is 100 percent complete. This lets the lender know that its collateral and its loan are exactly where they should be.

Fixed-rate mortgage. A mortgage with an interest rate that does not change throughout the term of the loan.

Float. An active decision not to "lock" or guarantee an interest rate while a loan is being processed. This is usually done because the borrower believes that rates will go down.

Float down. A mortgage loan rate that can drop as mortgage rates drop. There are usually two types of float, one being used during the construction of a home and the other during the period of an interest-rate lock.

Foreclosure. The bad thing that happens when the mortgage isn't repaid. Lenders begin the process of forcefully recovering their collateral when borrowers fail to make loan payments. The lender takes your house away.

Freddie Mac. Federal Home Loan Mortgage Corporation (FHLMC). A corporation established by the U.S. government in 1968 to buy mortgages made in accordance with Freddie Mac guidelines from lenders.

Fully indexed rate. The number reached when a loan's index and its margin are added together. This is the rate on which an adjustable-rate note is determined.

Funding. The actual transfer of money from a lender to a borrower.

Gift: When buying a home, a situation in which the down payment and closing costs come from someone other than the borrower instead of coming from the borrower's own accounts. Usually such gifts can come only from family members or from foundations established to help new homeowners.

Ginnie Mae. Government National Mortgage Association (GNMA). A government corporation formed by the U.S. government to purchase government loans like VA and FHA loans from banks and mortgage lenders. Think of it as Fannie or Freddie, only it buys government loans.

Good faith estimate. A list of estimated closing costs on a particular mortgage transaction. This estimate must be provided to the loan applicant within 72 hours after the receipt of a mortgage application by the lender or broker.

Hazard insurance. A specific type of insurance that covers homeowners against certain destructive elements, such as fire, wind, and hail. It is usually an addition to homeowner's insurance, but every home loan has a hazard rider.

HELOC. Home equity line of credit. A credit line using a home as collateral. The customer writes a check on the line whenever he needs it and pays only on the balances withdrawn. It is much like a credit card, but secured by the property.

Homeowner's insurance. An insurance policy covering not just hazard items, but also other things such as liability and personal property.

Impound accounts: Accounts set up by a lender to receive the monthly portion of annual property taxes or hazard insurance. As taxes or insurance comes up for renewal, the lender pays the bill using these funds. Also called "escrow accounts."

Index. The basis for establishing an interest rate, usually with a margin added. Almost anything can be an index, but the most common are U.S. Treasuries or similar instruments. See *fully indexed rate.*

Inspection. A structural review of the house that looks for defects in workmanship, damage to the property, or required maintenance. It does not determine the value of the property. A pest inspection looks for things such as termites, wood ants, and so on.

Intangible tax. A state tax levied on personal property. An intangible asset is an asset not in itself but because of what it represents. A publicly traded stock is an intangible asset. It's not the stock itself that has the value, but what the stock represents in terms of income.

Interest rate. The amount charged to borrow money over a specified period of time.

Jumbo loan. A mortgage that exceeds current conforming loan limits.

Junior lien. A second mortgage or one that is subordinate to another loan. This term is not as common as it used to be. You're likely to hear simply "second mortgage" or "piggyback."

Land contract. An arrangement whereby the buyer makes monthly payments to the seller, but the ownership of the property does not change hands until the loan is paid in full. This is similar to the way an automobile loan works: When you pay off the loan, you get the title.

Land to value. An appraisal term that calculates the value of the land as a percentage of the total value of the home. If the value of the land exceeds the value of the home, it's more difficult to find financing without good comparable sales. Also called "lot to value."

Lender policy. Title insurance that protects a mortgagee from defects or previous claims of ownership.

Liability. An obligation on the part of the borrower. Liabilities can be those that show up on a credit report, such as student loans or car payments, but they can also be anything else that one is obligated to pay. It's the ones on the credit report that are used to determine debt ratios.

Loan. Money granted to one party with the expectation of its being repaid.

Loan officer. The person typically responsible for helping mortgage applicants get qualified; she assists in loan selection and loan application. Loan officers can work at banks, credit unions, or mortgage brokerage houses or for bankers.

Loan processor. The person who gathers the required documentation of a loan application for loan submission. Along with your loan officer, you'll work with this person quite a bit during your mortgage process.

Lock. The act of guaranteeing an interest rate for a predetermined period of time. Loan locks are not loan approvals; they're simply the rate your lender has agreed to give you at loan closing.

Margin. A number, expressed as a percentage, that is added to a mortgage's index to determine the rate the borrower pays on the note. For example, suppose the index is a six-month CD at 4.00 percent and the margin is 2.00 percent. The interest rate that the borrower pays is 4 + 2, or 6.00 percent. A fully indexed rate is the index plus the margin.

Market value. In an open market, the value of a property that is both the most that the buyer was willing to pay and the least that the seller was willing to accept at the time of contract. Property appraisals help justify market value by comparing similar home sales in the subject property's neighborhood.

Mortgage. A loan on property where the property is pledged as collateral. The mortgage is retired when the loan is paid in full.

Mortgage-backed securities. Investment securities issued by Wall Street firms that are guaranteed, or collateralized, by home mortgages taken out by consumers. These securities can then be bought and sold on Wall Street.

Mortgage insurance (MI). An insurance policy, paid for by the borrower with benefits paid to the lender, that covers the difference between the borrower's down payment and 20 percent of the sales price. If the borrower defaults on the mortgage, this difference is paid to the lender. MI, also called "private mortgage insurance" (PMI), is typically required on all mortgage loans with less than 20 percent down.

Mortgagee. The person or business making the loan.

Mortgagor. The person(s) getting the loan; the borrower.

Multiple Listing Service (MLS). A central repository where real estate brokers and agents show homes and search for homes that are for sale.

Negative amortization (neg-am). An adjustable-rate mortgage that can have two interest rates, the contract rate or the fully indexed rate. The contract rate is the minimum agreed-upon rate that the consumer may pay; it is usually lower than the fully indexed rate. The borrower has a choice of which rate to pay, but if the contract rate is lower than the fully indexed rate, the difference between the two payments is added back to the loan. If your contract payment is only $500 but the payment at the fully indexed rate is $700 and you pay only the contract rate, $200 is added to your original loan amount. This is not for the faint of heart or for those with little money down.

Nonconforming. A mortgage loan in an amount above the current Fannie Mae or Freddie Mac limits. Also called "jumbo mortgages."

Note. A promise to repay. There may or may not be property involved, and it may or may not be a mortgage.

Origination fee. A fee charged to cover costs associated with finding, documenting, and preparing a mortgage application; usually expressed as a percentage of the loan amount.

Owner's policy: Title insurance for the benefit of the homeowner.

PITI. Principal, interest, taxes, and insurance. These figures are used to help determine front debt ratios.

PMI. Private mortgage insurance. See *mortgage insurance (MI)*.

Points. See *discount points*.

Prepaid interest. Daily interest from the day of the loan closing to the first of the following month.

Prepayment penalty. A monetary penalty paid to the lender if the loan is paid off before its maturity or if extra payments are made on the loan. Prepayment penalties are sometimes divided into "hard" and "soft" penalties. A hard penalty is an automatic penalty if the loan is paid off early or if extra payments are made at any time or for any amount whatsoever. A soft penalty lasts for only a couple of years and may allow extra payments on the loan, as long as they do not exceed a certain amount.

Principal. The outstanding amount owed on a loan, not including any interest due.

Realtor. A member of the National Association of Realtors. This is a registered trademark; not all real estate agents are Realtors.

Refinance. Obtaining a new mortgage to replace an existing one.

Sales contract. The written agreement, signed by both the seller and the buyer, to buy or sell a home.

Second mortgage. A mortgage that assumes a subordinate position behind a first mortgage. If the home goes into foreclosure, the first mortgage must be settled before the second can lay claim. Sometimes called a "piggyback" mortgage.

Secondary market. A financial arena where mortgages are bought and sold, either individually or grouped together into securities backed by those mortgages. Fannie Mae and Freddie Mac are the backbone of the conventional secondary market. Other secondary markets exist for nonconforming loans, subprime loans, and other types of loans.

Seller. The person transferring ownership of and all rights in a home in exchange for cash or trade.

Settlement statement. A document that shows all financial entries during the home sale, including sales price, closing costs, loan amounts, and property taxes. Your initial good faith estimate will be your first glimpse of your settlement statement. This statement is one of the final documents put together before you go to closing and is prepared by your attorney or settlement agent. Also called the Final HUD-1.

Survey. A map that shows the physical location of all structures and where they sit on the property. It also designates any easements that run across or through the property.

Title. Ownership in a property.

Title exam/title search: The process by which public records are reviewed to uncover any previous liens on the property.

Title insurance. An insurance policy that protects the lender, the seller, and/or the borrower against any defects in title for or previous claims to the property being transferred or sold.

Index

Look for These Exciting Real Estate Titles at
www.amacombooks.org/realestate

A Survival Guide for Buying a Home by Sid Davis $17.95

A Survival Guide for Selling a Home by Sid Davis $15.00

Are You Dumb Enough to Be Rich? by G. William Barnett II $18.95

Everything You Need to Know Before Buying a Co-op, Condo, or Townhouse by Ken Roth $18.95

Make Millions Selling Real Estate by Jim Remley $18.95

Mortgages 101 by David Reed $16.95

Real Estate Investing Made Simple by M. Anthony Carr $17.95

The Complete Guide to Investing in Foreclosures by Steve Berges $17.95

The Consultative Real Estate Agent by Kelle Sparta $17.95

The Home Buyer's Question and Answer Book by Bridget McCrea $16.95

The Landlord's Financial Tool Kit by Michael C. Thomsett $18.95

The Property Management Tool Kit by Mike Beirne $19.95

The Real Estate Agent's Business Planner by Bridget McCrea $19.95

The Real Estate Agent's Field Guide by Bridget McCrea $19.95

The Real Estate Investor's Pocket Calculator by Michael C. Thomsett $17.95

The Successful Landlord by Ken Roth $19.95

Who Says You Can't Buy a Home! by David Reed $17.95

Your Successful Real Estate Career, Fifth Edition, by Kenneth W. Edwards $18.95

Available at your local bookstore, online, or call 800-250-5308

Savings start at 40% on Bulk Orders of 5 copies or more!

Save up to 55%!

For details, contact AMACOM Special Sales

Phone: 212-903-8316. E-mail: SpecialSls@amanet.org